Stay Focus!

Scott

Additional Praise
for *Camera Focus*

"What a perfect metaphor: through the lens of photography, *Camera Focus* teaches us about business, life, and success. Today we all carry around amazing little "cameras" in our pockets thanks to our smartphones, to capture those Kodak Moments. *Camera Focus* speaks to anyone that might have distractions in their life, and we all live with some form of distractions. Scott Proposki has a unique way of using familiar photography terms like Aperture, ISO, Shutter Speed, and Color Balance and apply them to our everyday struggles between distraction and focus."

— Marc Jourlait, CEO, Kodak Alaris

"*Camera Focus* is your light at the end of the tunnel. If you are feeling lost – whether it be in your business or personal life – this book will help you find your true passion and show you how and where to focus your time and efforts so that you can do what you love. This will be the best gift Santa delivers on Christmas day, be sure to add this book to your list."

— Mitch Allen, Hire Santa, (as seen on Shark Tank, NBC)

"At first glance, one might think this book is a book about photography. Dig a little deeper and see that *Camera Focus* is a business book for people who might get bored early into most business books, a lifestyle guide for people who shy away from "self-help," and a memoir for anyone tired of finding inspiration but little practical advice in the life stories of others."

— **Richard Russey, VP, Publisher of Inc. Magazine**

"I find Proposki's personal stories easy-to-read, and I love how each one is turned back to the reader to connect the dots between your story and the focus point of the chapter. Easy to relate to, even though I have never had a near drowning experience in Mexico, or gotten stuck in the snow. Proposki brings the reader full circle, tying each chapter up with a pretty bow and reminding them what the bigger picture is, whether in life or in business."

— **Sara Bielinski, Small-Business Owner**

"If you have ever felt disorganized, *Camera Focus* is your book and your tool. Scott Proposki shows you how you can focus your efforts and finally take control of your time, your passions, and your work all to see the big picture!"

— **Ted Leonard, CEO Photobucket,**
The Worlds Largest Photo Sharing Innovator

"Anyone that is looking for strong focus, *Camera Focus* is the book for you. All of our customers are photographers and have a strong passion about photography. Scott's unique book, with his metaphor around the camera, will help many people everywhere find more focus. We look forward to sharing this book with our customers."

— **Doug Schirripa, President, Image Tech Marketing**

"As a small business owner building cedar log furniture in Maine for nearly thirty years, I found *Camera Focus* inspirational in gaining more focus in running my business day-to-day. Scott's storytelling style of his personal experiences really makes applying his insights into the business so much easier. A must-read whether you're just starting your first business or you've been in business for decades."

— **Mark Cross, Entrepreneur**

CAMERA
FOCUS

CAMERA FOCUS

What **Photography** Teaches About *Business*, *Life*, and *Success*

SCOTT PROPOSKI

Redwood Publishing, LLC
(Orange County, California)

Redwood Publishing, LLC
info@redwooddigitalpublishing.com
(949) 829-BOOK (2665)

Ordering Information:
Quantity sales. Special discounts are available on quantity purchases by corporations, associations, and others. For details, contact the publisher at the email listed above.

Printed in the United States of America (Orange County, CA)

Published and designed by: Redwood Publishing, LLC
(www.redwooddigitalpublishing.com)

ISBN Hardcover: 978-1-947341-55-5
ISBN Paperback: 978-1-947341-53-1
ISBN eBook: 978-1-947341-54-8

Library of Congress Cataloguing Number: 2019936434

10 9 8 7 6 5 4 3 2 1

Acknowledgments

First and foremost, I want to thank everyone I have ever focused my camera lens on to take your photo—you are the ones that made me Camera Focus.

I am grateful for everyone who has supported me over the years—my family, my friends, and my customers who have turned into my dearest friends. I am very appreciative of my coaching community at The Strategic Coach—there, I am surrounded by incredibly amazing people. Their energy has been contagious and has driven me to a higher level than I could have ever imagined.

I have spent many months writing my ideas to create the book you hold in your hands today. I could not do any of this without the help of my unique team at Photos In A Minute and the exceptionally gifted editors who keep me focused on every deadline.

Thank you to Sara Stratton, my publisher at Redwood Publishing for taking this project on. Your coaching words from our first call have been amazing. I am looking forward to launching our next series of mini books and workshops together—The Camera Focus Vision Builder™.

Thank you to my wife, Melissa Proposki, who might have thought I was joking when I said I was going to write a book on that summer day in July. Thank you for letting me share my story that will indeed help others in the future—mission accomplished!

Lastly, thank you to my parents. I am genuinely grateful to have you both in my life for the past fifty years and I am looking forward to many more joys in our lives in the epic years ahead.

Contents

Foreword
By Graham McFarland

Scott Proposki and I are cut from the same cloth. Not only do we share a passion for photography, we also share a little corner of the business: event photography. Currently, my passion has led me to Cherry Hill Programs, which is the world's largest provider of seasonal photography. If you've taken your children to get a photo with Santa Claus or the Easter Bunny anywhere in North America in the past decade or so, you've probably seen our work.

I met Scott nearly twenty years ago when he was a customer of my software company, Express Digital. My company developed some of the earliest software for digital cameras, then an emerging technology. Specifically, we created a program that facilitated communication between digital cameras and digital printers. Our software allowed photographers to have a printed photo minutes after it was taken. As Scott would say, it was "photos in a minute."

Scott was one of our early success stories. Our software was especially valuable for people who were photographing live events, from sporting matches to senior proms. A large part of Scott's business at the time was just that kind of photography. Not only was he a customer, he quickly became a friend as well. He even went on to mentor several other new clients, showing them how they could also use our software to enhance their businesses.

Growth is a struggle for any entrepreneur, but especially for photographers. Expanding beyond one's immediate market is a major branding and promotional challenge. At the particular time when Scott and I met, it was even more difficult. Photography as a discipline was undergoing a major shift from film to digital. A lot of people failed to anticipate the speed of that change and found themselves scrambling to keep up. Scott was one of the few who were able to see where photography was headed, and changed his business model accordingly. What he's done with Photos in a Minute wasn't really possible in the age of film, and because he recognized that, he was among the few who were actually able to take their businesses from the local to the national stage. I've been in the photography industry for twenty-five years, and in that time, I can count on one hand the number of people who've matched Scott's success.

The switch to digital was just the first of several seismic technical shifts in professional photography. In the decades since, there have been unprecedented changes, not just in terms of camera work, but also in how businesses are launched and run, and how the consumers themselves engage with photography. When everyone has a digital camera and photo-editing capabilities in his or her pocket on a smartphone, how does professional photography stay relevant as a business?

Scott has been able to continually reinvent himself and his business, adapting to new realities and staying one step ahead of the crowd. A lot of photographers get lucky once or twice: they happen to be really interested in or good at some aspect of the discipline that suddenly becomes popular, and they are able to capitalize on that. Scott has been better than lucky; he has been proactive. He has been able to foresee upcoming shifts in the industry, and more importantly, he has been willing to innovate. His vision and adaptability have made him a mainstay in an industry that all too often turns on a dime.

Scott cites me as a mentor, but I think our mentoring relationship goes both ways. I can't count the number of productive, energizing conversations we've had over the years. Most of them have had one central theme, one vital to anyone looking to be more than they are at this moment: What will the future look like, and how do we solve problems that are worth solving? With this book, Scott has distilled those ideas into a useful, easily readable guide to anyone in any industry.

The lessons Scott has learned and the skills he has perfected are about much more than just taking pictures. His thoughts on growth, change, risk, and perspective are the result of years of hard work and firsthand experience. Though his journey has been unique, the conclusions he has reached are broadly applicable. Whether you are a photographer or a personal trainer, a veterinarian or a restaurateur, we all struggle with growing our careers, envisioning the future, and developing the focus and skills necessary to make that future our reality.

CHAPTER 1

I've Always Been Focused on the Camera

If you asked most of my teachers in school who among their students was most likely to write a book someday, I'm pretty sure I would have been near the bottom of the list—if I made the list at all. When it came to the classroom, I generally tried to keep as low a profile as possible in order to avoid drawing attention to how much I struggled to focus on what I was supposed to be doing.

Have you ever seen one of those TV strongman competitions in which modern-day barbarian warriors compete to see who can pull some enormously heavy object with some unexpected body part that isn't designed to do that? When it came to schoolwork, my mental process felt an awful lot like trying to pull a monster truck with my gritted teeth.

My report cards featured mostly Ds, with the occasional C to spice things up, and that was good enough for me. If I passed a class, even narrowly, I considered it a job well done. It never really occurred to me that I could, or should, ask for help. I took it as a given that I was just not good at school, and I thought if I approached my teachers about my struggles, it would only draw attention to my poor performance.

In addition to my academic issues, I was also a shy kid—which might surprise anyone who met me as an adult! I didn't like to talk much in class, and I was never the type to raise my hand and volunteer. Instead, I always preferred to stand back and observe the action from a safe distance. For a lot of people who knew me then, the notion that I would ever be willing to put my own story out in the world in book form would have seemed crazy.

There was one person, however, who was always convinced that I had a book in me . . . and that was my father.

It started when I was little more than a teenager. Whenever something unusual or interesting would happen to me, Dad would say something like, "I hope you're taking notes for your book." At first, I assumed he was joking—who would read *my* book?—but as I got older, I realized he was serious.

Once, early in my career as a photographer, I had to go to New York City for a job. It was an exciting opportunity, but I was nervous about trying to get around in NYC. I'm from the suburbs of Boston, so I'm no stranger to big cities, but I've never been much of a navigator, and New York was unfamiliar to me.

This was also in the mid-1990s, well before GPS devices were in common use, so I relied on the old-school version of those services: a skilled navigator riding shotgun. On this trip, that navigator was my father, who would painstakingly plan our route on a paper map the night before, and then give me directions as I drove.

As we made our way through the crowded city and I struggled to get around unexpected street closures, impassible traffic, and darting pedestrians without losing my way or missing our appointment, my dad chuckled and said once again, "This will be a great chapter for your book."

Usually, when he said something like that, I just nodded and laughed. In that instant, though, I realized he was serious. He really thought I was going to write a book, and that this part of my life would be an interesting inclusion. I wasn't sure exactly how to feel about this epiphany—I certainly had no intention of writing a book at that time—but it definitely didn't feel *bad*. Dad believed in me; he saw something in me that no one else did, and that made me wonder if *I* hadn't been missing something as well.

I've always looked up to my dad. I'm the youngest of three, and for whatever reason, Dad and I have always had an especially close relationship. We're alike in many ways, but as I grew older, there was one central shared interest that cemented our bond: photography. Dad worked as a photographer for the Honeywell corporation in Lawrence, Massachusetts, but it wasn't just a job for him; it was also his primary hobby. He built a darkroom in the basement of our modest suburban home in South Lawrence, Massachusetts, and in this darkroom he would develop his film and print photos, which he would hang there to dry.

Photography is in my DNA: My cousin Richard Pineau, a person I always looked up to, worked at Polaroid in Cambridge, Massachusetts, and my uncle Roger Culliford was a corporate photographer for AT&T back in the eighties.

As soon as I was physically capable of it, I was down in the darkroom helping my dad every chance I got. When I think about my childhood, I recall the unique chemical smell of the fixer we bathed the undeveloped images in, and how it would stain my hands if I wasn't careful. To me, the process was like magic, except that it was real and I could do it myself in my own basement. Before my very eyes, I could conjure images from blank Kodak paper like I was materializing them out of the air. I still keep a photo from those days with me in my writing notebook. In it, I'm about seven years old, and I'm holding up a little chart to help my father adjust his settings for the perfect exposure.

Quickly enough, I graduated to taking pictures of my own (mostly headshots and portraits) and developing them along with Dad's prints. Inside that darkroom, I was so completely focused and engaged that the world outside of it felt a little bit less real and urgent. After a night of working on my photography, I would spend the next day at school daydreaming about what technique I wanted to try next, while the teacher's instructions faded into a dim background hum. Photography was endlessly fascinating to me; when I was working with a camera, everything just felt *right*, like it was what I was supposed to be doing.

Positioning myself behind a lens was also a great way to maintain that observer position that I'd always preferred. Like a lot of professional photographers I've met, I quickly established myself as "the one with the camera" at family functions. It gave me a job (so no one would try to rope me into extra chores), and it allowed me to do something I genuinely enjoyed during an event that would have otherwise taxed my ability to sit still and follow long conversations. In the seventies and eighties, family gatherings were one of the few occasions when people commonly took photos.

The seventies were also the heyday of a new device, one designed to make photography more accessible and more integrated into the average family's lifestyle: the instant camera. When you think of an instant camera, you almost certainly think about Polaroid; they dominated the early market for so long that we still often call instant, self-developing photos "Polaroids." Throughout the sixties and seventies, Polaroid was constantly innovating and refining their instant camera system to make it easier and faster. As a corporate photographer, my dad would often get the latest

> Photography felt *right*, like it was what I was supposed to be doing.

Polaroid camera for his work, and he would always bring it home first to test it.

I loved playing around with the Polaroid; I enjoyed the immediacy of being able to hold a fully developed photo in my hand almost as soon as I had snapped it. "The photo will be ready in a minute," Dad would tell me after I took a picture. "Go shake the trays in the darkroom, and it'll be done when you get out."

That phrase, "photos in a minute" kindled something in me. It was so evocative of that magical feeling—that feeling of conjuration—that had drawn me to photography in the first place. Years later, when I had to settle on a name for my business, the choice was immediately obvious to me: "Photos in a Minute."

The instant camera was a big part of my transformation from "the kid wandering around with a camera" to "the official family photographer." I kept all the pictures I took in a little collection along with my other photography projects, and at a family get-together one year, I brought out all the shots I'd taken at other family gatherings. I thought it was a cool example of how my skills had evolved over the years, and how the technology itself had changed during that time—but I wasn't prepared for how engaged my family members became. They pored over the pictures, recounting old memories and laughing about events from years past.

I had always understood what photography meant to *me*, but that was the first time I saw how important it could be to people on the other side of the camera. I had captured something—a moment or a feeling or a memory—and had created a physical object to preserve it.

The older I got, the more I cemented my identity as "the camera guy," and eventually even people who didn't know me well knew that I loved photography. Still, I was surprised and a little alarmed when my high school's guidance counselor, Mrs. Parker, summoned me to her office one day during my senior year. My strategy of keeping my head down and rarely drawing attention to myself had worked in the sense that although I was still only barely passing my classes, I'd never actually seen the inside of the guidance counselor's office in my entire time at Lawrence High School. I couldn't imagine what our counselor could possibly want to talk to me about, but I naturally assumed it somehow had to be negative.

I can still remember the overwhelming scent of Pine-Sol emanating from the freshly washed hardwood floors as I fidgeted in the hard seats outside Mrs. Parker's office. Was it about my grades? Was I not going to be able to graduate? Had I somehow done something wrong or gotten in trouble without realizing it? I inventoried all of my activities in recent memory, and none seemed particularly nefarious.

Finally, Mrs. Parker opened her office door and invited me in with a smile. I took that as a good sign. If she was smiling at me, it couldn't be that bad, could it?

She greeted me warmly, though I couldn't remember ever having interacted with her before this moment.

"Scott, you like to take photos, don't you?"

I nodded, still a little confused. This was about photography?

"Well, this year we're thinking of doing something a little different for graduation. We'd like to put together a slideshow of photographs from the entire year and project it during the ceremony. Do you know how slides work?"

"Of course!" I replied.

At the time, the Kodak Carousel slide projector was extremely popular, and like most photographers, I'd tried my hand at creating 35 mm slides. (I could never have imagined that thirty-five years later, I would be collaborating with the CEO of Kodak and discussing the future of the company with him!)

"That's wonderful to hear. We were hoping you'd be willing to take photos this year at sporting and other school events so we can collect those pictures and present them as a slideshow at the end of the year. Is that something that interests you?"

It took all of my self-control not to leap out of my seat and shout "Yes!"

Instead, I offered her a very serious and thoughtful "Sure, I could do that." Inside, however, I was buzzing. It was my first real "job" as a photographer, and the parameters of the job were wide open; all that really mattered was that I deliver a compelling slideshow in time for graduation.

There were also some fringe benefits to my new position as the semi-official school photographer. For one thing, I now had an institutional green light to do what I would have done anyway: focus entirely on my camera. My graduation project was treated basically like another class, and I was even permitted to miss or drop other classes to have more time to take photos.

I also discovered that my camera was now a skeleton key to pretty much anywhere I wanted to go. All I had to do was drop Mrs. Parker's name and gesture to the camera around my neck, and no one paid me any mind. Backstage at the school play, in the announcer's booth at the basketball game, down the field during the homecoming game—any place that seemed interesting was now open to me because of those magic words: "I'm the photographer."

But I wasn't just using my project as an excuse to goof around; I was genuinely interested in getting the best shots and building a killer presentation. The slideshow consumed my year, and I spent most of my time in school either strategizing or walking around, grabbing candid photographs of classes in session and students engaged in various activities. Most of my free time was devoted to attending a slew of after-school events to make sure I got adequate coverage of them for the show. I took many, many pictures, and spent hours sorting through them endlessly to find just the right one for each moment. It was painstaking, often repetitive work. Yet, even as I flipped through dozens of pictures of the same three-point shot or trombone solo, I never had trouble keeping my mind on the task at hand. Somehow, when the work was photography, it didn't feel much like work at all. In fact, I sometimes had to force myself to take breaks, or I would wind up spending half the night looking through pictures and forget to sleep.

In the end, my efforts produced a slideshow that was, as we say in Boston, wicked cool. And if you ask anyone from the Lawrence High School graduating class of 1988, I imagine you'll probably hear the same. For years, whenever I ran into someone from high school, even someone I hadn't really known, he or she would always mention the slideshow.

Novelty was probably part of the appeal; it was the first time the school had done a presentation like that, and they'd sprung for a nice, large projection screen so the images looked bigger than life. But people also liked the show for the images themselves. I'd gotten some good shots, but more important, I'd gotten *unexpected* shots. I didn't limit myself to the traditional yearbook categories or styles (partially because I wanted to be comprehensive if I was going to represent our whole year, and partially because the more stuff I found to photograph, the less time I had to devote to regular classwork). In practice, this meant that people who weren't used to seeing themselves in school-related media were included maybe for the first time—and even people who did expect to be photographed weren't necessarily expecting to see the moments I chose to memorialize.

> When the work was photography, it didn't feel much like work at all.

I scored the presentation to a song I was obsessed with at the time, Michael Jackson's "The Way You Make Me Feel." For as long as I can remember, I've regularly gotten "stuck" on songs or albums, pieces of music that I'd listen to over and over again. Often I'll get stuck on one particular song or album during a specific project, and the two things will become linked, either because the song in some way informs the project or simply because they both occupy the same time in my life.

I remember my high school buddy Ken Hamm questioning my song selection and asking me, "Why Michael Jackson?" That year I was very into Michael Jackson in general. I had read somewhere about the singer's struggle with vitiligo, a disease that causes the gradual loss of pigment in one's skin, often in patches. Vitiligo was the impetus for a lot of the fashion choices that Michael was criticized for, including the heavy makeup and the constant use of gloves and other concealing garments. As a person of color, vitiligo was particularly noticeable in Michael's case, and all his attempts to hide it or distract from it only seemed to draw more scorn.

As a teenager, with a teenager's insecurities and fears, I strongly connected with that fear of having all one's flaws visible to be dissected and judged; I, myself, had vitiligo. Michael was one of the most visible people in the world in the late eighties, and yet I saw in him the same impulse to hide that had led me to pick up my camera. I listened to his entire discography that year, connecting more with certain songs than others at particular times, but from the beginning, the slideshow presentation *was* "The Way You Make Me Feel," so it only seemed right to use it in the finished product.

Sitting there in the darkened auditorium, watching my images flash on the screen to Michael Jackson's unmistakable tenor, I knew I'd made the right choice. How could I have imagined then that my passion for photography would someday lead me to the opportunity to meet the King of Pop himself, Michael Jackson (and numerous other celebrities), in person?

When I think back on my career, I realize it's impossible to say exactly when it "all started." Was it that first time I toddled down to the darkroom to see what Dad was doing? Was it when I brought my camera along to that first Thanksgiving or Christmas gathering? Was it the first job that actually paid me? I can never know for sure, but I know that my senior-year project, and that moment of culmination in the auditorium, was a pivotal step. We were all sharing something as we looked up at the screen and watched the memories drift by, and I knew that this was what I wanted to do with my life.

After graduation, it never really occurred to me to try college. I knew I didn't have the grades, and the only thing I really wanted to learn more about was photography. I was pretty confident that the best way to get that knowledge was to keep doing what I was doing—and ideally, to try to get paid for it. I started working as soon as I could, and one job just seemed to lead very naturally into the next.

Before I knew it, those jobs began to get better and more prestigious. From photographing Fox Networks' holiday parties in New York City with sexy Santa elves (those photos were published in the *Wall Street Journal*—a long story that we'll get into later) to shooting for the National Geographic Society, Miley Cyrus, and the White House, I took everything one step at a time and found that, like links in a chain, those individual jobs had become a career.

As I write this today, I am forty-nine years old, and it may surprise people to learn that I didn't really start thinking analytically about my career until just a couple of years ago. I've spent most of my professional life simply focusing on the immediate task in front of me—what did the client need and how was I going to provide it for them—and I've rarely stepped back to take a look at the larger picture.

The impetus for the change really came from two intertwined decisions I made. The first was to investigate Strategic Coach®, a training and skill-building program for successful entrepreneurs. It was in Strategic Coach that I first learned about the concept of Unique Ability®, a specific skill every entrepreneur brings to the table that makes him or her valuable to the general market. Finding your Unique Ability is one of the foundational lessons that Strategic Coach uses to guide aspiring entrepreneurs, and without realizing it, I'd already been doing that. As it turned out, there were many components of the Strategic Coach program that I had already employed in my professional life, having discovered them either by accident or instinct.

When I started speaking with Dan Sullivan, the creator of Strategic Coach, he was impressed with how much I had accomplished without any real model or formal education. I didn't know anyone who had started his or her own company at the time that I did it myself, and I certainly didn't have the benefit of an MBA or any other business degree. I'd done things by trial and error, and I'd definitely had some bumps in the road, but for having gone it pretty much alone, I'd done very well. It was gratifying to hear that, and to hear Dan's analysis of the choices I'd made and why they worked—or didn't work. Without really thinking about it, I'd come to approach these business decisions almost automatically; I always just went with my first impulse. Seeing it from Dan's perspective, I could finally see how significant even seemingly simple decisions had been for building my business.

Dan and I spent a lot of time together. I would always seem to find a way to hang out with him at his company-coach café in Toronto . . . something that people ask me about all the time: "How did you do that? Did you have an appointment?" No, I just sat down and we began to talk. For some reason, Dan made that time for me, and I'm grateful.

One day Dan offered an important observation, one that would transform my life. As he began to speak, I could tell he was treading lightly.

"Scott," he said, "I mean no offense with this question, but I wanted to ask you: Have you ever been tested for ADD?"

It was reasonable that he'd been a little gun-shy about asking. ADD—now better known as ADHD, or attention-deficit/hyperactivity disorder—occupies a pretty odd position in American culture. It's the most commonly diagnosed learning disorder, and it's estimated that 5 to 7 percent of the population has the condition in some form (though estimates vary widely from country to country, and even from state to state). Still, ADHD's actual incidence is dwarfed by its cultural visibility—and unfortunately, most of what people have heard and believe about ADHD is wrong.

Even medical professionals and scientists are still learning about how ADHD works, and much of the information that has made it into popular consciousness is incomplete, outdated, or flat-out wrong. Americans on the whole have misconceptions about almost every element of this disorder, from how it works, to what the symptoms are, to who can be diagnosed, to how it can be treated, and even whether it really exists at all. Saying that someone has or "is" ADD or ADHD is often an insult or a punch line, similar to the way that someone who has a really organized desk might jokingly call themselves "OCD." Many people would have taken a question like Dan's not as a genuine inquiry, but rather as a judgment of their behavior or personality. For too many of us, "Do you have ADD?" often translates to "What's wrong with you?"

When Dan asked me that question, I had about as much knowledge of ADD as the average layperson—which is to say, almost none. My first reaction was to wonder, *Isn't that what they medicate little kids for when they can't sit still in school?*

"I believe that many, maybe even most entrepreneurs have ADD or ADHD," Dan told me. "It's the characteristic that often makes for creative people who get bored easily and need constant challenges—which is basically the profile of an entrepreneur. I've had a lot of clients who came to me diagnosed or received a diagnosis while we were working together, and I have to say, I see a lot of those traits in you."

I wasn't sure what to think, but I trusted Dan's judgment, and his reasoning seemed sound. He pointed out some things about me that I had always thought of as just personality quirks: how I struggled to remember names and dates but had perfect recall for the moments that most interested me, how I was always losing paperwork and documents, how I jumped from project to project when one started to get difficult, and how I focused narrowly—almost obsessively—on photography to the exclusion of everything else. After all, wasn't that why I was talking to him in the first place? Because only now, after twenty years of building my business, was I starting to develop myself and my entrepreneurial skills instead of just my camera proficiency?

I never knew that the personality traits Dan was describing could be symptoms of ADHD; I thought the problem was that people couldn't focus at all, not that they focused too much. I always figured that some people were just good at organizational tasks, and that some, like me, simply weren't equipped for that sort of thing. But Dan's words stuck in my head, and I started thinking more seriously about seeing a psychiatrist and getting evaluated.

Of course, as was typical for me, I procrastinated; it took me another year to actually make that appointment. But as soon as I started talking to Dr. Barnard, my psychiatrist, things began to fall into place. At the end of that first session, he looked at me and said, "Scott, it is 100 percent indisputable that you have ADHD. We could do a formal examination, but I think that would be a waste of everyone's time. My biggest question, honestly, is how much Adderall we should try you on to start."

I was a little dumbstruck. As we were talking, he kept jotting down things I said (especially when I talked about how many times I'd tried and failed to make the appointment, and how I was fifteen minutes late because I'd characteristically gotten lost while trying to find parking), but I still thought I was just describing my personal habits and foibles. But as he explained to me later, those things were actually well-known symptoms of ADHD.

It felt strange and uncomfortable, like trying on a rented suit that didn't quite fit, but at the same time, there was something compelling about it. All my life, I'd thought of my struggles as the result of choices I'd made or a lack of effort: I couldn't remember things because I didn't care enough about them. I couldn't pay attention in school because I didn't really want to. I invested all of myself in one project because I didn't want to risk failing in other areas of my life. Now someone was telling me that there was a reason things were so hard for me, that my brain was actually absorbing and processing information in a different way than "normal" brains do.

My second feeling was one of embarrassment. "Do I have to tell anyone?" was the first question out of my mouth when the psychiatrist had finished talking. Even the diagnosis of ADHD provided some answers about my life and experiences. It also had some shameful connotations. I wasn't just a forgetful or disorganized person; I was someone who had something wrong with me. ADHD is also often placed under the umbrella of "learning disabilities," and it made me wonder if people would think less of me when they heard I had it. Would they assume I was intellectually handicapped as well? The fact that ADHD was so strongly associated with schoolchildren also made me feel like, as a nearly fifty-year-old man, I should have "grown out" of my symptoms.

"No," Dr. Barnard said gently, as though he'd heard this question many times before. "You don't have to tell anyone if you don't want to."

We then talked about treatment options, about how I was feeling, and about life in general. As I was getting ready to leave, he stopped me and said, "Scott, I want to let you know something. I see some pretty significant symptoms of ADHD in you, things that would make life challenging for anyone, and I think you should take some time to reflect on what you've been able to do considering that. Many people with ADHD do creative work and have high IQs, but I would say that you have been even more successful than the average undiagnosed and untreated person. You've obviously created a unique product and a unique service, and I think it's important to acknowledge the hard work and skill that went into that."

What he said struck a chord with me. He was getting to the heart of some of my fears: that something was wrong with me, that people would think of me as incapable, or that I was, in fact, simply unable to do many things at all.

"I hope that someday you will reconsider your decision not to tell people, Scott," he added. "You have nothing to be ashamed of. On the contrary, I think your story could change lives if you're willing to tell it."

Again, I heard my father's words in my head: *Make sure to put that in your book.* In that moment, I wasn't ready to share my experience with anyone outside my most immediate circle, but a seed was planted that day, one that would eventually grow into the book you are now reading.

It took years—decades, in the case of my father—but I finally believe the people who told me I had something to share with the world besides my photographs. But this book isn't just about my experience as someone with ADHD, or as an entrepreneur, or even as a photographer. It's a fusion of all those things, a collection of all the lessons I didn't even realize I was learning, and those that I've only been able to understand in retrospect. It's a guidebook for anyone who dreams of something bigger and isn't quite sure how to bridge the gap, and it's a story about creative passion and making the thing you love work for you. For anyone who struggles with endemic personal or institutional challenges, it is a message: You are not alone. I see you, I acknowledge your struggle, and I am here to tell you from personal experience that success, fulfillment, and even joy *are* possible for you.

Camera Focus is a guidebook for anyone who dreams of something bigger and isn't quite sure how to bridge the gap.

As you read this book, I would like you to begin imagining the future you want for yourself. Think about how you would feel in that future—how you would fill your days and what would occupy your attention. The image may be dim or a little bit fuzzy at first, like the blobs and blurs that initially appear in a freshly snapped Polaroid, but be patient. Come along with me now, and we'll see what develops.

CHAPTER 2

– The Right Lens –
Be Great at Just One Thing

We all know what a "good" photo looks like. Or at the very least, we know the difference between a good one and a bad one. Is the subject in focus? Is the subject in frame, or have pieces of it been unceremoniously chopped off? How about the lighting: is it too dark to make out details, or are those details blown out with light? These are some of the most obvious and immediate ways we judge an image, and in general, they are pretty reliable indicators of a photographer's experience and competence. But when we look beyond simple competence, it can be much harder to pinpoint what separates the merely "good" images from those that are truly great.

The most obvious tells for a bad or inexperienced photographer are a result of misusing or misunderstanding the equipment. Basic photography is about mastering the tools of the trade, learning how the parts of a camera work together to produce an image, and being able to manipulate the scene to get your intended shot. The next level is about learning how to make choices with those tools, and this is where we begin to see an individual's personal stamp on his or her work.

In my experience, career and personal development follow a very similar trajectory. First, you get the lay of the land, find the tools available, and figure out what they do. You practice with those, getting better by small increments, and then, by the time you're seeking out a book like this, you are ready to ascend to that next level of difficulty. In almost any circumstance, it is the intersection of tools and knowledge that fuels excellence.

When I talk about how the choices we make with the tools we have spell the difference between "just OK" and "truly great," I think immediately about lenses. In photography, selecting a lens is one of the first choices you make on a project, and this choice informs all the others. Each lens has individual features—like different focal lengths and aperture sizes—that will make for wildly different photographs of the same subject. A good photographer weighs all the possibilities before making a final decision.

But, of course, the other side of the equation is the subject of the photo. Being able to make good choices isn't solely about the hardware you have at your disposal; it's also about understanding what you are trying to capture in your image: What feeling are you trying to evoke? What kind of experience do you want people to have when they look at your pictures?

> In career and personal development, you get the lay of the land, find the tools available, and figure out what they do.

For example, consider what should be a pretty easy choice to make: Do I use a micro lens designed to show the finest details of tiny objects, or do I use a wide-angle lens that can encompass an enormous scene? These choices are complete opposites; surely there's no way that both could be appropriate for a single project, right?

Let's say I'm photographing bees, and I want a picture that communicates to a viewer something about the nature of bees. My first instinct might be, *Use the micro lens; it's for small things, and bees are small.* But let's think a little deeper; bees *are* small, but they are also creatures of collectives. One could make the argument that using a wide-angle lens to take a shot of a large swarm of bees would tell the viewer something just as important about bees and the quality of "bee-ness" as an extreme close-up of a bee landing on a flower. Even with the same subject, different lenses make for different outcomes.

Lenses are also vital in our personal and professional lives; many people don't realize we have a choice about the prism through which we see the world. Everyone has a perspective, though we are rarely so conscious of it as we are when selecting a 14 mm versus a 50 mm lens. And the thing about choosing a lens is, once you make that choice, you've gotta commit to it. The moment you photograph something is the last moment your subject exists in that exact form. Everything is always changing, even if only in the smallest ways, and once we snap that picture, we can never truly go back for a redo. That's why I think the first question anyone has to ask him- or herself when trying to make a breakthrough, either personally or professionally, is *What lens am I using?*

If we were using Strategic Coach's parlance, this would be known as identifying your "Unique Ability®," but I like to use the lens metaphor because I think it adds an important layer of meaning to the idea. It's not just about discovering what you can do for others, but also about understanding how you see the world in your own specific way and being able to effectively communicate that vision to others. A good lens—the *right* lens—bridges the gap between the ideas inside your head and the real world.

In my case, my primary lens has always been photography—but more specifically, it has been the unique combination of immediate gratification and memorialization that is event photography. I chose the name of my business, "Photos in a Minute," more or less on instinct, remembering my dad's instructions to me in our basement darkroom—but as my career grew, that idea became my guiding principle.

As I write this, I am working to roll out my big holiday feature, The Santa Experience, to dozens of locations nationwide. As the name implies, The Santa Experience is designed to be more than just a picture with Santa Claus:

> The *right* lens bridges the gap between the ideas inside your head and the real world.

each child gets a meeting with the big guy, a keepsake, and a certificate, as well as incredible photos to take home and cherish. When I first started out, there wasn't really a name for what I was doing with this combination of entertainment and photography. Event photography, as a discipline, has grown with me, and it is the most effective tool I've found to share that vision with the world—and the perfect lens to get the shot I need.

Though I hit upon the seed of Photos in a Minute at a very young age, it would be decades before I was able to consciously understand and describe my "strategy" for developing my career. When I was younger and less experienced, I fell into a common trap of thinking that professional growth could only be achieved by adding features rather than deepening and perfecting one skill. Most memorably, I briefly tried to add wedding photography to my repertoire. On the surface, it seemed like a logical extension of what I was already doing with other types of events, but in reality, wedding work is a whole different animal. The more I looked into it, the more I realized that it involved a kind of people management and, well, ceremony that didn't really gel with my skills or my vision. I also found that the people who really make wedding photography work spend a huge amount of time networking and growing their businesses. I had initially thought of it as "weekend work," but really there is an enormous amount of market research and advertising that goes on outside of the actual gigs.

Wedding photography is a great business, but it wouldn't have been great for *me*, and realizing that early on saved me a lot of heartache in the long run. I actually credit my ADHD with helping me to stick to the path that was working for me. Despite the name, ADHD is not really about a lack of attention or focus so much as it is an inability to *direct* one's attention. Among the more pronounced features of ADHD are an inability to fully visualize rewards in the future, and an overwhelming desire for mental stimulation. In practice, that means that people with the disorder really struggle to complete tasks that aren't immediately beneficial or exciting to them. (This is a big part of why I always did so poorly in school.) On the flip side, when someone with ADHD is interested in something, he or she can become practically obsessed with it, a phenomenon known as "hyperfocus." This extremely narrow and intense interest in one specific thing is often mistaken for mania, and some people with hyperfocus report forgetting to eat, sleep, or tend to many other self-care basics while in the throes of a particularly compelling project or idea.

In high school, when I was spending almost all my free time laboring over the graduation slideshow, that was a classic example of hyperfocus, though obviously I didn't know it at the time. I was lucky in that the thing that gave me the greatest burst of excitement and pleasure was photography instead of, say, video games or impulse shopping. Because my area of focus was useful, I didn't experience many of the downsides of hyperfocus, and was able to enjoy some of the benefits. I've never been good at pushing myself through something that I don't find compelling, and in my professional life, that has been an unexpected blessing. If I were perfectly neurotypical, I might have tried for years to force myself into wedding photography, but I would never have been passionate about it—and in a creative field, that means the work suffers. Moreover, all the mental and physical energy I would have poured into growing a wedding-photography business would have had to be pulled from somewhere else—almost certainly from the work I actually liked doing.

Too often, people get caught up in feeling like they have to be full-service providers. They tear themselves apart trying to be all things to all people instead of zeroing in on one specific thing and doing it impeccably. In terms of lenses, this would be the equivalent of a photographer stopping to change the lens after every shot, which would result in him or her getting a quarter of the shots a more consistent shooter would get in the same amount of time.

A few years ago, my wife and I took a vacation to Reykjavik, Iceland, where I got an object lesson in the value of specialization. While there, we visited an online friend who happened to do local tours, and he offered to show us around. It was an incredible trip, full of stunning scenery and wonderful people, virtually all of whom were wearing those big knitted Icelandic sweaters with the ornate patterns around the neck and chest. It seemed like these sweaters were standard issue for Iceland—sort of how everyone in New York seems to own at least one black leather jacket. So I finally asked my host where I could buy one, because, obviously, it was the thing to do!

"Oh," he said easily, "my wife makes them."

I was a little surprised, and even more surprised when he invited us to come back to his place and look at some of her wares. I also got to see an incredibly skilled and focused artisan at work; my guide's wife had been knitting sweaters by hand for more than forty years. As I looked at some of the sweaters she'd made, I began to recognize the patterns and the craftsmanship; I was pretty sure that several of the people I'd seen wearing sweaters around town had been sporting her work. She had a thriving, long-term business doing one very specific thing that she loved. They say it takes ten thousand hours to become proficient at anything; imagine how skilled she was after four decades!

I think of the Icelandic sweater spinner whenever I get the sudden urge to add something completely different to my business. *Is this really the best use of my abilities,* I ask myself, *and will it help me realize my vision?* Usually the answer to both questions is no.

But picking the right lens, finding the tool that best suits your abilities and your goals, is about more than just saving time and effort; it's also about creating confidence. When you know that you have the right lens in place, when you are sure that what you are doing will bring you closer to realizing your vision, that knowledge creates an unmatched sense of assurance. After all, if someone simply handed you a random lens and told you to make do, you'd be a lot less certain of the outcome than if you'd gotten to carefully select one yourself.

In one of those vicious cycles so common to human growth and development, however, it appears that people actually need a certain amount of self-confidence to be able to identify their lens in the first place. If you can't believe in yourself and your judgment, it's very hard to trust your own perspective and chase your vision. Again, I am oddly fortunate in that ADHD made it nearly impossible for me to do anything other than my passion, but many people have difficulty seeing their enthusiasms as important and instructive. Yet we are still drawn to the things we love, even if we try to suppress them or paper over them. Often, when I work on helping people discover their unique skills and vision, I find that the answer is already in their lives, usually from a very young age. If we could only buy into those early passions and nurture them from the beginning instead of fighting them in the name of what we "should" do, imagine how much time and energy we would have to put toward our goals.

Over the course of my career, I've worked with a lot of high-profile people who do creative or otherwise unusual work, often for a global audience. Their jobs are high stakes and high visibility, and it takes a certain level of confidence to be able to get to the positions that many of these folks occupy. One thing all my various subjects have in common, whether they're movie stars or politicians, is certainty about their vocations. Most of them have felt that certainty for as long as they can remember, and one of the most interesting parts of my career has been getting to watch these individuals perform at different times in their career. I've seen people go from fresh-faced newcomers to superstars, and the most successful of them felt that certainty right from the beginning.

One event in my life that really crystalized this idea for me was a photo shoot I did years ago for ABC. The assignment was to photograph a Disney Channel star during a live musical performance. As an adult with no kids, I had no idea who this person was, though I was assured that her show was very successful and this photo shoot was part of her push to transition into music.

For my part, I was mostly focused on the technical details of the job. It was a big, complex project, and I had to have a lot of things set up just right if I was going to be able to get the shots I needed. I brought my dad along to help with preparations, just as I always did. At one point, while I was setting up equipment, Dad came over holding what appeared to be a diamond-studded microphone. He looked a little confused.

"Dad," I said, "what are you doing with that?"

He shrugged and held it up so it glittered under the lights. It was a really fancy microphone, definitely not something we'd brought along.

"Oh, that long-haired guy over there gave it to me." Dad paused and cracked a small smile. "He said I've gotta hold on to it, because it's gonna be in the Smithsonian one day."

My seventy-year-old dad, who spent his free time doing photography experiments in his basement, was probably the only person there less familiar with the Disney Channel and its stars than I was. He rolled his eyes.

"I told him, '"Sure, buddy, I'll take good care of it.'"

I chuckled, already thinking about the play of lights on the microphone and how best to incorporate it into my plan for the shoot.

"Well, whatever you do," I told him, "don't lose it!"

Dad agreed, and we finished our preparations with no further surprises.

As it turned out, that "long-haired guy" who had alerted my father that he was holding a future museum piece was one Billy Ray Cyrus. He was there along with his wife and daughters to oversee the shoot, and it was his daughter Miley whom I would be photographing.

More than once, Billy Ray commented to whoever was listening that this was just the beginning for Miley, and that she was going to be a superstar musician someday. When Miley herself appeared, she certainly performed as though that were true. There was an assured quality to her singing that seemed beyond her years, and she played to the audience with the confidence of a seasoned performer.

In the years since, Miley Cyrus's career has exploded and evolved, and whenever one of her songs comes on the radio, I think back on that day. I wonder what role that confidence played in Miley's success—not just her own confidence, but also her father's. What could we be if we had people in our lives who supported and reflected our ambitions from an early age? I think of Miley the way I sometimes think about elite athletes or scientific prodigies: almost anyone who becomes a world-class anything starts at a young age and has someone around them who is willing to help them chase a passion. What is the impact of having your vision validated from the beginning, even before you embark on the necessary years of training and practice? What would you be able to do if you didn't have to first overcome your doubts about your own instincts?

In some ways, I had a Billy Ray of my own. My dad always supported my interest in photography, and he always believed in my business. And yet, somehow, that didn't banish all my personal doubts. Maybe it was the flip side of the way ADHD made it so difficult to succeed outside my focused interest. I often felt that I was investing my life in photography not because it was the best thing for me to do, but because it was the only thing I *could* do. I'd so often used my camera to avoid situations where I knew I'd struggle or even fail. Maybe my career trajectory wasn't based on my having chosen the right lens; maybe there had been only one lens in the bag.

Dan Sullivan coaches a workshop that is based on his "4 C's Formula®." Dan believes that every entrepreneur needs to make real breakthroughs: Commitment, Courage, Capability, and Confidence. I've often struggled with the Confidence part of that formula: How can I be sure that my choices are correct? How can I be sure that what I'm doing will propel me forward? It's easy to let these kinds of thoughts derail you. I've found that the best way to banish these worries is to step back and take a look at the bigger picture.

A few years ago, I went down to Panama City during spring break to photograph a concert headlined by another musician I knew nothing about, this time, a country singer named Luke Bryan. You may be familiar with him now, as he's had some top-selling albums since then and gets a lot of play on the country

> Every entrepreneur needs Commitment, Courage, Capability, and Confidence to make real breakthroughs.

stations—but at the time, he was just starting out. Neverthe-less, this guy owned the stage from the moment he appeared. He was clearly giving every song his all, and the crowd was incredibly responsive. Never at any point did he give the impression that he was expecting any other reaction.

Wow, I thought to myself, *I wish I had that kind of confidence.* Maybe it was because I was in my mid-forties, wearing a schlubby T-shirt and jeans while standing in a sea of excited twenty-somethings in their bathing suits, but I just couldn't imagine getting up in front of the world and doing a thing like that. I couldn't imagine having no fear of judgment or mass disapproval. *He's got what it takes to be a star,* I thought, because, for me, that was what being a star meant: it was being willing to practice your passion no matter who was watching.

The very next day, I actually had another photo shoot, this one for *Maxim* magazine. I was photographing their model of the month, Katrina Bowden, for *Maxim*'s Spring Break Party event. I was onstage with her in front of a huge audience, but it actually took me until about halfway through the shoot to really process that fact. Thousands of people were watching me work and I hadn't really even noticed. I had been so focused on the job—on my final vision—that I hadn't even spared a thought for all the eyes on me. It was in that moment that I realized I *did* have the confidence of a Luke Bryan. With the camera in my hands and a job in front of me, I knew exactly what I had to do, and it didn't matter if the whole world was watching. To commemorate the moment, I even had another photographer snap a photo of me onstage with the audience visible behind me. When I look at that picture, I see in myself something that I've seen in so many other subjects over the years: the peace that comes from knowing your purpose.

A lens, when used properly, doesn't just reflect how we see the world; it can actually *change* how we see the world. The right lens can show us details or a larger context we'd never see with our naked eye. It can create a mood or a feeling, or it can link seemingly unrelated images or concepts. In fact, anyone who wears glasses knows that sometimes a lens is necessary to make the world comprehensible. When you find that lens, the tool that allows you to see the world with clarity and work without fear, hold on to it. It will be the way you make your mark on the world.

CHAPTER 3

– Aperture –
Getting the Right Exposure
for Yourself

In the simplest terms, an aperture is a hole that lets in light. In photography, when we talk about the aperture of a lens, we are talking about the size of that hole, and by extension, how much light it will allow to reach the image plane of the camera (this is the area where the film—or in a digital camera, the image sensor—is located). The lens aperture, along with a couple of other settings we will talk about later, determines the exposure of an image. Exposure is what makes an image an image—without that interaction between the light and the image plane, there's no photograph—and gradients of exposure also often make the difference between good and bad images.

The concept of the aperture is an excellent metaphor for building our careers: just as with photography, exposure in our professional lives must be carefully managed. Too much light ruins an image by obliterating all the details, while too little light renders those same details invisible in the darkness. Similarly, professional exposure is a balancing act. Tip too much to either side, and you'll end up obscuring the image you wanted to project.

Aperture is also a useful metaphor because it's all about *what you let in*, a concept that is especially important in the digital age. When we talk about exposure today, we are talking largely about online exposure, and the online environment is a place where, in theory, everyone gets to decide how much of themselves they will make visible. In reality, however, threading the needle of a successful digital presence is difficult for people who aren't also representing a business. The internet gives us an unprecedented ability to share with the world, but it's very easy to make a mistake, and mistakes online have a way of spiraling out of control. That's why it's so important to have a strategy and goals before we start developing our reputations, either online or in the physical world. So, before any *#branding* takes place, ask yourself what your aperture settings should be.

The challenge in this question, however, is that different projects require different apertures. There's no rule of thumb for how much light you want to let into an image in every situation. Every picture is different, and depending on what effect you are trying to achieve, you could be justified in using apertures of wildly different sizes.

> Just as with photography, exposure in our professional lives must be carefully managed.

For example, if you are trying to get a clear picture at dusk with limited light, you could use a fairly large aperture because you are trying to let in all the available light. Think of the way our pupils dilate in a dim room; our eyes are working like a camera and trying to capture the minimal light. Similarly, if you are in an environment with very harsh or bright lighting, you probably want to use a small aperture to avoid drowning the image in white. If you've ever seen your pupils shrink rapidly in the sun—or been briefly blinded when going from a dark room into full sunlight—you've experienced this adaptation in action.

There are many other rules of thumb for various situations: Smaller apertures are generally used for landscape shots, and aren't usually favored for close-up images of people. Wider apertures are considered better for isolating and highlighting just one subject. And there are countless other basic guidelines. As you become more comfortable playing with your settings, you can also begin to manipulate your exposures in other ways, such as changing the shutter speed, in order to create cool effects like the long, dynamic trails of light and movement we get from long-exposure photography.

The key considerations are:

1. What final vision am I trying to achieve?
2. What are the ambient conditions?
3. How do those first two considerations interact?

When I consider how to apply all those concerns to building name recognition, I think of how I met one of my most important mentors, Graham McFarland, eighteen years ago. I knew of Graham because he had invented some of the first and most significant software for event photography. Graham's work basically created the concept of an event photographer, which meant that he basically created my job. Long before I met him in person, I admired and appreciated his work, which promised to make the creation and printing of photos nearly instantaneous. So when I heard he was doing a presentation of his software at a conference in Chicago, I immediately bought a plane ticket.

As it turned out, on the weekend of the conference, a huge storm hit Chicago, and I'm not talking about a little rain. As I settled into my taxi at Midway International Airport, the radio was warning that a tornado had touched down nearby. The radio then blared the emergency broadcast signal and encouraged listeners to take shelter.

The cab driver shot me a look in the mirror and asked, "You sure you still wanna go to a hotel?"

All I could think was how important it was that I learn about the software that seemed to be the key to making my "Photos in a Minute" vision a reality.

"Yeah," I said. "I still wanna go."

When I arrived at the hotel, the conference was proceeding as normal, but it looked like a lot of the other attendees had decided not to brave the storm. The room where Graham was speaking had been set up for about two hundred people, but only three, including me, had actually made it.

Graham himself was still there, though, and he gave his presentation with gusto. He laid out how the software worked, but more important than that, he explained how it was going to change the future of photography. He addressed us as though he were playing to a packed auditorium rather than to a group that wouldn't have filled an elevator.

After the presentation was done, Graham caught my eye and asked, "Wanna grab a beer?"

"Absolutely," I replied.

I had been intrigued by his work even before the presentation, but now I was sold. It wasn't just his clear, cogent explanation and his vision for the future; it was the way he seemed to be living in that future. He had a certain clear-cut plan for his career, and he conducted himself accordingly, even in situations in which he probably could have gotten away with presenting himself much less professionally. He could have looked at his "crowd" that day and decided to cancel, or simply sat and chatted with us instead of walking us through his work patiently and professionally. But that was not the picture of himself that Graham wanted to present, and while he couldn't control the circumstances of the situation, he could still control his own aperture settings; he didn't have to switch to unprofessional mode just because he didn't have the audience he might have wanted.

As we chatted at the bar, I peppered him with questions, and he answered each question only after giving it careful consideration. That conversation, and the presentation that preceded it, convinced me to buy his software. I cut him a check right there at the hotel bar. I didn't even think twice about the six-figure price tag, and as it turned out, I was able to make that money back in just three months with Graham's program. Just as he had promised, it revolutionized my company.

I've talked with Graham a lot in the years since then, and I've always found him to be just as conscientious and solicitous as he was that day. No matter what he was working on—and as a brilliant innovator, he was often very busy—he always took the time to speak with me and provide meaningful answers to my questions. Graham had a vision of the future, not just for photography, but for himself as well: he saw himself as a resource for people in the industry. Because he so consistently presented himself in this way, that image of him was cemented in my mind—and I'm sure in the minds of many others.

When I started developing an online presence for myself, I thought a lot about Graham's strategy of looking to the future and behaving as though that future was already here. I was a relatively early adopter of social media because I foresaw its importance in the future, and I invested early in creating a digital resume for my business and myself.

"Creating my digital resume" didn't just mean making samples of my work available online, though that was part of the equation. It also meant that I did other things that would be recorded, observed, or catalogued online. My digital resume is not my portfolio or the photosinaminute.com domain I bought; it is the first page of Google results that appears when you search for my name. There you will find the usual suite of social media accounts, but you will also find links to presentations I've given at conferences, schools, and other public forums. There are video links and transcripts along with descriptions of the organizations I've spoken to, and of course, a summary of my own work and career.

Soon I began to build links between the concepts I discussed and my own name and business. If you search for keywords like "event photography" or "instant photos," you will find my appearances and speeches—and by extension, my company.

For a long time, I did this reflexively, like I did a lot of my career building. Whenever an opportunity came up, I took it, and that was how I wound up doing a lot of these conferences and workshops. It was very similar to the way I accepted paying work: if it was on the table, I was going to make a grab for it. The fact that these events were slowly building an identity for me online was pretty incidental to my decision-making process, however, and it took an actual crossover between the digital world and the physical one to show me just how important my online presence had become.

At one point, I was entering into an RFP (Request for Proposal) process for a large company. Essentially, this meant that the company was looking for a certain service and had opened the floor to pitches from a number of companies, including mine. I was to explain how I would tackle the job and why my unique approach was the one that would be successful for them. It was a somewhat high-pressure process, as it involved way more selling than I generally did in my daily life. By this time, a lot of my biggest clients were actually coming to *me* because they were already familiar with my work, so they didn't need to be wooed in quite the same way.

Answering an RFP also tends to involve multiple rounds of presentations as companies are eliminated and the choices are winnowed down. Eventually, I was invited to pitch to a high-level team at the company's New York office. This was the big one; my success there would probably determine whether Photos in a Minute was granted the coveted contract.

I spent the whole night before going over my slide presentation and refining it. I nitpicked every word and reconsidered every image; I practiced every gesture and aside until I felt like I could do them in my sleep. I tried not to be nervous, but it was tough not to feel the pressure. When I arrived at the company's office on the fifty-second floor, it was hard not to feel as though the city stretched out below me was watching as well, just waiting to see if I would triumph or flop.

Everybody settled into their seats while I set up my equipment, and a young man who introduced himself as Ryan asked me about the time I'd photographed the White House Easter Egg Roll. "What was it like photographing President Obama and his family?" he asked.

At first, I was a little thrown—he was talking to me like we were old friends although we'd never met before in my life. But after I answered his question and a couple of follow-ups, I began to feel an incredible sensation: relief. Suddenly it felt like I had a friend in the room, and I began to orient myself toward that feeling. Instead of launching into my polished, mechanical speech, with its carefully placed pauses for gestures and jokes, I started a conversation with the people in the room.

We talked about my work, and about my more fascinating experiences, including doing promotional photography for HBO's *Game of Thrones*, and the White House Easter Egg Roll, which had been interrupted by an active-shooter emergency. But we also touched on my philosophy, both in terms of photography and work. When a conversation about fishing led to a discussion about the difference between "Free Days" and "Focus Days," I explained how I structured my life to maximize my ability to focus, and how the Entrepreneurial Time System® that Dan Sullivan created—a system in which one's days are split up into Free, Focus, and Buffer Days®—helps me to be more creative and more effective.

I was able to actually speak to the parameters of their job and how I would approach it, but I allowed that information to come out in an organic way. Instead of a lecture, the whole thing became more of a Q&A, as each question led into some other element of my work. As we talked, I began to feel my jitters being replaced by a sense of peace. The RFP, the competition, the job itself—it all kind of faded into the background as I concentrated on forging an actual connection with the people in that room and being able to talk meaningfully about the things I cared about.

In some ways, it was the opposite of what Graham had done all those years ago at that Chicago hotel. Instead of maintaining structure and formality even in the face of a casual audience, I had chosen to go with a more personal approach in a setting where others might have relied on a practiced script. But the difference in our individual approaches is unimportant: what Graham and I were both doing was understanding the person we wanted to be . . . and *being* that person. In my case, that meant being direct and personal, even informal.

After the presentation, Ryan came up to congratulate me on what he called "the best sales presentation I've ever been to," and I asked him how he'd known about my other work.

"Oh," he said, "I'm the intern. It's my job to research anyone who comes in here to make sure they are legitimate.

You passed all the tests, but I loved reading about your projects online, and I couldn't wait to meet you."

It was in that moment that I realized I had been building a brand and identity for myself online for years, albeit only semiconsciously. Ryan talked to me like a friend because that was how I had presented myself in other speaking engagements and on social media. I had come into that office worrying about whether I'd picked just the right wording or work samples, but in practice, all I had to do was take my own lead. For years, I had been setting out the image of who I wanted to be for my clients and associates; now all I had to do was live up to it!

Since then my online presence has only grown, but I've done my best to maintain that same open and personable tone. The nature of social media makes it impossible to get a three-dimensional picture of someone else's life—everything you see has been edited, curated, and selected to present some sort of image—but I think the difference between people who use social media in positive ways and those who fail to use it effectively is that the former have a clear sense of what picture they are trying to present.

For me, it is important that I be as authentic as possible. I want people to know that anything I post on Facebook or Instagram is a legitimate thought I had and wanted to share, not a thinly disguised promotion or fakery of some experience I never had. And if I do promote something, I want it to be a real thing—a true bullet point on my digital resume. So I might share a story written about me in the *Wall Street Journal,* or a talk I gave that appeared on YouTube, but I don't want to relentlessly flog every mention of my name. I also work hard to make sure that the ratio of "promotional" content to personal content is well-balanced. I want people to feel like they are following a real human being, not a brand with a marketing department that is brainstorming tweets all day.

It's also important to me that my social media presence be generally positive. While I do want to share my thoughts and experiences, I don't want to use the internet to work through the hard parts of my life. I try not to bring an angry or sad energy to social media because that's not something I would bring to a job. Too often, social media can feel a constant feedback loop of drama, rage, and depression, so a little sunshine here and there does not go unnoticed.

I also want to be willing to have the kinds of discussions I had with Ryan and his colleagues in New York. That meeting demonstrated to me the incredible power of starting a dialogue with people, even if it seems tangential to my actual work.

The key to having a useful internet presence is to shape it meaningfully, just as you can play with the aperture setting of a camera to get that perfect image. The worst thing you can do is just jump in without a plan and without any boundaries in place; that is how you end up with nothing but a blur. When I think about professional overexposure, I think about people who don't seem to have any overarching vision for what they want to put out in the world, so they just share indiscriminately and wind up presenting a muddled mess.

The first rule of avoiding overexposure is avoiding bad exposure. And, yes, some people will tell you that there's no such thing, and there are some isolated cases in which people have done unconscionable things and managed to capitalize on that notoriety in some way, but I don't consider that a viable approach. Not only are such things ultimately self-limiting (if you're known for some awful stunt, your primary value is no longer your work; it's your status as a curiosity), but I also think it's just a bad way to live your life.

I believe your digital identity should be roughly 70 percent "real stuff"—meaning work you have done, or presentations, papers, lectures, or any other supplementary things you've done to establish yourself—and only about 30 percent social media ephemera. I often see people flipping those percentages, but the prettiest Instagram in the world can't make up for a lack of concrete professional history or the lack of a meaningful perspective. The first step toward building your brand is to actually do the work. If you do it well and put your name on it, that gives you a firm foundation to build upon, and more often than not, the rest of your web presence will fall into line with that foundation.

> The key to having a useful internet presence is to shape it meaningfully, just as you can play with the aperture setting of a camera to get that perfect image.

Another good way to avoid exposing too much or the wrong parts of yourself is to consider everything you post in the context of your ultimate vision for yourself and your company. We've all seen people put black marks on their professional reputations by flying off the handle over a bad review or leaving a nasty comment on someone else's post. I can guarantee you that those people were not thinking, "Yes, this expletive-laden tweet is exactly how I would present myself to a potential customer" before they pressed "enter." Remember, the internet may seem like it's "not real life," but it is the most public forum there is. If you wouldn't say something in a room full of current and possible customers, then don't say it on Facebook, because that is exactly who your audience will be. And just as a small difference in your aperture size can ruin a photograph, even one digital slipup, if it's significant enough, can fundamentally change your image in the eyes of countless others.

The last and most important rule of thumb for managing your exposure is to recognize that it will be an ongoing process with continual changes to anticipate and accommodate. When we think about the aperture in terms of photography, we are also thinking about a moving target. The light is always changing, sometimes in ways we can't even fully appreciate with our human eye, and it's a combination of experience, technical knowledge, and instinct that allows a good photographer to make the changes they need to make before the next noticeable change.

This is not a skill that is unique to photography, either. Once, my team was working on an all-day shoot for the New England Patriots at Gillette Stadium in Foxborough, Massachusetts. We were on the fifty-yard line all day, but just being in one place didn't mean we spent the whole day doing the same thing. We had to constantly adjust the aperture to accommodate the changes in light, the different desired focus of each shot, the movement we were trying to capture, and the scope of the image we wanted. At one point, it occurred to me that someday, maybe even the next day, Tom Brady would stand right where I was and make crucial adjustments of his own. He would be thinking ahead, trying to anticipate what the other team would throw at him, and moving players around as needed. Tom Brady would be thinking, just as I was, about how exposed he wanted to be—and how sheltered. He would be making educated guesses about conditions in the future and trying to respond to those conditions before they arose.

Nothing remains static, not on the football field or in the sky overhead, and definitely not online. You will need to do as Graham suggested to me all those years ago, and keep your eyes fixed on the future. But beyond that, you will have to be able to make regular adjustments to meet that future. That combination of skills—seeing ahead and taking action in the moment—is what will ensure that your vision emerges crystal clear.

CHAPTER 4

– Viewfinder –
Seeing the Bigger Picture

Many years ago, I attended a trade show where I saw a new kind of viewfinder whose creator told me was designed specifically for headshots. A viewfinder is a tool—usually built into the camera but sometimes a separate piece of equipment—that helps a photographer compose his or her shot. Looking through a viewfinder, the photographer can see the scene *as the camera sees it* and plan accordingly. Many people imagine that photography is about just looking through a camera lens and determining how well focused or well positioned the subject will actually be in the photograph.

Viewfinders often also feature markers or overlays that allow photographers to see your "stats" (the current settings you have applied) or the points on the image where the camera is going to focus. Some more sophisticated overlays divide the scene into sections, which helps the photographer make sure that his or her final shot is visually balanced. The viewfinder I saw at the trade show that day had a suggested crop that was intended to highlight single-subject portraits.

Most images are cropped in one way or another after the picture has been taken, either when they are printed or before they are shared online. Photographers crop to highlight a subject, to make a picture less visually chaotic, or even to correct bad framing in the original shot. What this viewfinder did was show the photographer how the image would look with a given crop before the photo was taken. This meant that I would be able to frame and shoot with the ultimate end product clearly visible rather than trying to reverse engineer the photo I wanted from an imperfect existing one.

It was an appealing idea, and I decided to give the viewfinder a chance. At the time I'd been doing head shots intermittently, and I found that the new viewfinder transformed the way I approached those projects. Somehow, just seeing that suggested crop box on the screen changed the way I thought about the portraits I was taking. I began to focus on portraiture as a discipline, not simply as one more picture I needed to get on a given project. The viewfinder was a simple tool, but once I really understood what I was looking at, it allowed me to focus in an entirely new way.

It's been nearly twenty years since that trade show, and I still reach for that viewfinder when I'm working on a portraiture project. It's not just the actual function it performs; it's about the way it makes me think differently. The more I think about how we grow in our lives and careers, the more I am convinced that we all need to find our own viewfinders to help shape and refine our visions.

As someone with ADHD, I've had to think about focusing devices and adaptations perhaps more than the average Joe. Many people with ADHD or other executive-function disorders spend their lives finding or building viewfinders for themselves that let them see the most important part of a chaotic picture. Often we do this without consciously realizing exactly what we are doing or why. Once I was diagnosed, I saw much of my life in a different light, and I began to see how I'd been collecting viewfinders for myself over the years.

In my case, one of my primary viewfinders was a note-book—a totally basic pencil and paper set—that I've used to record and order my thinking at least since high school. I write down observations, reminders, plans, and ideas, and I even do drawings for concepts that are clearer to me visually than they are in words. If you looked at one of my notebooks, you would probably see a confused mess with no organizing principle, but for me, getting my thoughts on the page allows me to place them in a larger context. Inside my head, things zip around wildly, one idea sparking off another and leading me down endless rabbit holes. But once I write something down, it's fixed. I don't have to worry

> We all need to find our own viewfinders to help shape and refine our visions.

about forgetting it if I move on to something else, and it's easier to make those broader connections when I can see everything spread out before me.

The physical act of writing is important as well. Over the years, I've tried a number of other systems, from apps on my phone to a tablet (which I do find useful for lots of tasks), but nothing seems to work as well as old-fashioned pencil on paper.

I know I'm not the only one who gets something unique from the practice of writing. Several studies have shown that writing information down by hand makes us more likely to remember and retain that information. Physical note-taking aids in learning comprehension and later recollection, and there's some evidence that the connection between the motion of our hands and the process in our brains is critical to understanding and analysis. We are creatures of movement and energy, and research indicates that we understand the world best by interacting physically with it.

I've met a lot of people in my personal and professional lives who take a similar approach with notebooks of their own. Interestingly enough, I can often spot a person with ADHD by the contents of their book. Like mine, it's often seemingly disorganized and full of disparate ideas and concepts, with no particular style or structure of note-taking predominant. In many ways, these notebooks have become a way of externalizing our brains; the seemingly haphazard and crowded appearance mimics the extremely noisy headspace that so many people with ADHD experience.

The other class of people I've found who keep similar notebooks are high-level entrepreneurs and professionals. Some of them definitely overlap with the ADHD group, and their notes reflect that, but others keep very regimented books with clearly delineated topics and a clear system of organization. Many adhere to certain types of note-taking, like the Bullet Journal system or the Cornell method. While I think those specialized systems can work better for certain people, I think almost anyone can benefit from having a place to "brain dump" or workshop ideas. You should use whatever method works for you, but don't be afraid to go the freeform route and simply jot down whatever is on your mind.

These days, I think of my notebook as a "pocket coach." I use it not just to explore new ideas, but also to keep myself on track and energized. Taking even a few moments here and there to write something down or consult previous writings helps me center myself and gives me perspective, the same way that crop overlay in my viewfinder helps me visualize the final image a little more clearly. I'm also perfectly willing to bring out the notebook when I'm working through a problem or facing a decision with my team, a mentor, or even a client. I've found that I get a positive response to this practice most of the time; people are intrigued by the notebook and often remark that they should do something similar themselves—but for whatever reason, it just hasn't occurred to them before.

It's important to me that I be candid in this book about viewfinding tools like the notebook for the same reason that I've chosen to be frank about my experience with ADHD. There's a lot of pressure on people in any industry to be as self-sufficient and self-sustaining as possible. That's how even something as basic and innocuous as keeping a book to write down your thoughts in can be completely overlooked as an option; we are often trained to believe that we should be able to keep everything in our heads. A lot of time is lost dwelling on what we "should" be able to do rather than finding ways to work with what we *are* doing. It's important that we destigmatize these valuable tools that improve our lives and our work because tools are meant to be used and there's no shame in needing them. After all, no one would tell a photographer that they don't need a viewfinder because they should instead just get better at imagining what the camera is seeing!

I started keeping a notebook when I was around sixteen because it was a way of bridging gaps for me, either in my memory or in my ability to organize information, and I'm grateful that I was able to see those gaps and find a solution. I'm even more grateful, though, that I found that solution relatively early in my life. By the time I started really digging into the mechanics of how note-taking worked for me and why I was so drawn to it, I had been practicing it for almost three decades. I was able to build on an already positive practice instead of trying to create a new habit from scratch.

Not all the solutions we adopt are as good or healthy as note-taking, just like not all viewfinders are appropriate for every project. If I were to take my portrait viewfinder to photograph a sporting event or a vast wilderness scene, the information it gave me would be worse than useless; it would actively make for less clear and less interesting photos. Like many people with undiagnosed ADHD, I tried to fill other gaps in ways that were wrong, either for the situation or for me individually or for someone with my particular thought processes. Most often, these were solutions that worked at least a little bit in the short term but were destructive in the long run. The biggest "bad gap-filler" I found was the one that too many of us discover early in life: substance abuse.

People with ADHD are more likely than average to abuse alcohol and drugs, and there's a large overlap between ADHD and addiction. I personally struggled with this issue, and my behavior skirted the line between "unhealthy habit" and "full-blown addiction." My problems were the quiet kind, the kind that many Americans have, the kind that often aren't considered "problems" at all because most of us are able to meet our obligations and interact normally with the world. The fact that I drank a coffee mug full of Jack Daniels every

> Not all the solutions we adopt are good or healthy, just like not all viewfinders are appropriate for every project.

night, was fifty pounds overweight, and hadn't had a full night's sleep in years was just a personal quirk—my own business to sort out. This sort of lifestyle is extremely common among people with undiagnosed medical problems, and especially undiagnosed ADHD.

Part of the problem is that people with the disorder struggle with impulse control and crave sensation and immediate gratification. But I think a bigger factor is that so many of us are attempting to regulate our mental states on our own, with no guidance and no real understanding of our condition—or often, that we even *have* a condition.

Stimulants act differently on an ADHD brain. Instead of ramping us up, they often steady us and allow us to focus and shut out some of the ambient noise in our heads. That's why people with the disorder are often prescribed stimulant medications like Adderall and Ritalin, and incidentally, that's also where I think many of the misperceptions about ADHD medication come from as well. A neurotypical person who takes Adderall recreationally is going to have a totally different experience than someone who takes it as prescribed for a medical condition. One of the most easily obtainable and least stigmatized stimulants in our society is caffeine, and so a lot of undiagnosed people spend years using caffeine to get that feeling of focus and clarity. The problem with that approach (well, *one* of the problems) is that caffeine is not a good stimulant for treating ADHD. The effects tend to be short-lived, and tolerances build up quickly. Plus, people with ADHD can still suffer from the negative side effects of caffeine, like anxiety, jitters, and sleep disruption. In fact, anxiety can actually be compounded by ADHD, making the experience even worse than it would have been otherwise.

Before I was properly medicated, I self-medicated with caffeine—often with quite a lot of it because the work I needed to do always seemed to outstrip the amount of focus I could get from an "average" serving of caffeine. By the end of the day, long after the useful effects of the caffeine wore off, I struggled with anxiety, restlessness, and insomnia. I started drinking in part because I needed a depressant just to "come down" from all the caffeine I was consuming. But the occasional nightcap to take the edge off became a nightly ritual; the drinks got stiffer, and "just one" quickly turned into two and then three. You know where this story goes; it's the classic story of the functional alcoholic who is slowly becoming less functional and more alcoholic. And when I inevitably woke to a killer hangover the next morning, what was the first thing I reached for? If you guessed an extra-strong cup of black Starbucks coffee, you'd be right.

I had created a kind of Old-Lady-Who-Swallowed-a-Fly system. I was just constantly chasing equilibrium with one substance after another, and it took a major toll on my health. I never felt "good," only "good enough," and usually that meant "good enough" to meet my obligations and no better. Managing my eating and making time for exercise felt like impossible pipe dreams. This system of chemical dependence was a viewfinder of sorts, but the future vision it was showing me was all wrong for what I wanted. Instead of encouraging me to focus in a healthy way, the tools I chose were leading me further away from my goals.

These days, I use different things to help me see more clearly, and while I've maintained some practices I've always done (like note-taking), I've also pursued coaching and begun taking medication. Since being diagnosed, I've made behavioral changes as well: I've virtually quit drinking, cut my caffeine intake to a negligible amount each day, and lost forty-eight pounds. I sleep better at night, and the focus that I get from my Adderall regimen is of a completely different type than what I had before. Not only is it more consistent, lasting through the whole day, but also, I no longer have those spikes of intense focus that I would get with lots of caffeine. All too often, those spikes were followed immediately by blurry times when I couldn't seem to follow any thought through to its conclusion. Using caffeine the way I did was sort of like redlining your car—it will make you go a lot faster for a short time, but every time you do it, you are wearing down your engine. Getting properly medicated was like getting a whole new, much faster engine.

When Dr. Barnard put me on Adderall last year, he started me out on a very low dosage—five milligrams. That was all I wanted. I said, "I'm just going to try it out."

I took it, and it didn't take effect immediately—but when it did, it was like a bang, and everything went quiet. Up to then, my whole life had been about noise inside my brain. Now, for the first time in my life, I had quiet. Things slowed down. I could stay on track. I could stay on schedule.

Since then, I've had the most productive, creative year of my life, and it shows; everybody on my team notices it, and our clients stay with us for a long time.

Another hugely helpful change has been working with Dan Sullivan's Strategic Coach program. Not only is it designed for elite entrepreneurs, but also, it is based on Dan's own experiences, which in many ways dovetail with my own.

Much later in our acquaintance, long after I'd gone to see my therapist, Dr. Barnard, and begun taking my Adderall, I went back to the coach café at Strategic Coach and had a heartfelt conversation with Dan about my experience back home. When I asked him how he'd known I had ADHD, Dan in his wisdom looked me in the eyes and said, "You need to be one to know one." We laughed.

He hadn't told me earlier because he hadn't wanted it to color my thinking about my own situation, but he said that he felt Strategic Coach had even more to offer to someone with ADHD. Without realizing it, he had created a system that compensated for some of the weaknesses we have and capitalized on our strengths: creativity, intensity, and energy.

One example of this capitalization is the role that visualizing and preparing for the future plays in his system. People with ADHD have a complicated relationship with time; that is, our experience of time passing is different from the average person's. We have trouble estimating how long something will take or has taken. Often, we struggle to plan effectively because we can't connect our present moment with the future, and when you feel divorced from your future, it's impossible to work toward goals, delay gratification, and appreciate non-immediate rewards. Considering all that, you would think that a system built to encourage entrepreneurial growth—which requires one to think about the future—would be impossible for people with ADHD to adopt. But Dan Sullivan has found another ADHD trait that is very useful in projecting and planning: imagination.

One of the better-known positives associated with ADHD is creativity, and many people with the disorder have vivid imaginations and rich inner lives because of the unique way in which their brains work. In fact, getting too absorbed in one's internal fantasies (i.e., "daydreaming") is actually a common symptom of ADHD, especially for those of us without the hyperactivity component. When I would sit in class and run through possible photography experiments instead of absorbing the lesson the teacher was giving, that was a classic example of ADHD imagination in action.

What Dan Sullivan has done with Strategic Coach is devise a way for you to aim that imagination toward your future. One of the first questions he asks people who attend his workshops is, "How long do you plan to live?" Immediately, he forces us to imagine an end point, and from there, we begin to fill in the gaps. We become immersed in a world that doesn't yet exist . . . but *can* exist, if we make it happen.

I embraced this practice immediately because, like my notebooks, it was something that I'd been doing since I was a teenager. All I had to do was take that mental energy I'd been devoting to thinking through the various photographic approaches I wanted to try and redirect it toward business concerns. I conjured up an image of myself as clear as any "final photo" I aimed for when I raised my camera, but this image had to do with the structure and scope of Photos in a Minute. I kept one eye on that future, even as I navigated the present moment, because I realized that everything I was doing right now was leading me toward that vision.

I've always thought photography was a little bit magical, especially concerning the concept of time. A camera can halt time, preserve a moment forever. With a long exposure, a camera can show us the passage of time, written in the blur of a car's taillights or the trail a star makes as it moves across the sky. And when you think about it, having a viewfinder is a little bit like seeing into the future. Looking through a viewfinder means seeing the world not as it currently is, but *as it will be* after you've chosen your photo and allowed it to develop.

But there's really no such thing as "the future," is there? There's only a whole bunch of outcomes, any of which could come to be depending on the decisions we make in the present. A viewfinder offers one version of the future: a future with *these* specific settings and *these* points of light and *this* area of focus. A different viewfinder reflecting different choices might show you a completely different picture, and that's why it is so important to choose your viewfinder with care. When you find a tool or a structure that perfectly reflects what you need to meet your goal—in the way my portrait viewfinder makes for incredible headshots—you need to commit to what you see reflected there.

I've often joked that viewfinders and similar tools have become so advanced that photographers rarely even need to look through the lens; they can get all the information they need from the other displays. When you are able to clearly focus on your future, career building becomes a lot like that. As I write this, I am deep in the midst of the most hectic time of my year; like jolly old Santa himself, I am busiest during the Christmas season. But if you ask me what I'm thinking about—what is the actual vision that fills my head right now?—it's not the thousands of orders our team members

> Looking through a viewfinder means seeing the world not as it currently is, but *as it will be.*

are filling right now at each of our Santa Experience pop-up locations around the country, or even this book I'm writing, because I have already worked through those things in my head. Instead, I am considering the expansion of my business in the next five years, and what tools and team members I will need for that. I am also developing a plan to integrate this book and its message into my larger business strategy.

I am capable of acting and adapting in the present based on a plan that I've already put in place, but my creative, strategic mind is already on the next step. I can press the camera's shutter release without looking because I trust my viewfinder . . . and there is yet another future inside it now just waiting to be illuminated.

CHAPTER 5

– Shutter Speed –
How Quickly Will You Grow?

Harold "Doc" Edgerton, one of the early pioneers of high-speed photography, was not really a photographer at all. He was an engineer by trade and a tinkerer by inclination. He took up photography not as an artistic pastime, but as a means to perform experiments with light and motion. He wanted to capture moments that passed too quickly for the human eye to properly register them: the flicker of a hummingbird's wing, the expulsion of a bullet from a gun, the blast crater briefly formed when a drop of liquid hit a saucer of milk. Most famously, he created a photo called "Death of a Light Bulb," which memorialized the instant a light bulb was shattered by a .30-caliber bullet.

I was seven years old the first time I saw "Death of a Light Bulb." My father showed it to me before explaining that we were going to create something similar on our own. In our version of the iconic picture, it was a hammer that would strike the light bulb, as my dad wisely didn't want to fire a gun with his seven-year-old in our suburban basement. Still, everything had to be assembled with care because we would only get one chance at this shot (well, I suppose we could have had a few other chances, but sooner or later we would have run out of light bulbs).

We rigged the hammer to move when we pulled on an attached wire; that movement also triggered the camera's flash so the exact moment of impact would be captured on the image plate. We darkened the basement in preparation, and I waited with the same kind of nervous expectation I always got during the countdown to the new year.

When I think back on that experiment, I remember watching the glass of the light bulb explode and seeing the shards glimmer in the camera's flash . . . except I couldn't have seen any of that. That precise sequence of events—the action and reaction—occurred so quickly that I could not have visually registered the information before it was already over.

In reality, I probably experienced the light bulb breaking as a series of sounds: the crash of the hammer into glass and the tinkling of the pieces hitting the floor. In addition to the incredible speed of what was happening, the sudden flare of the camera flash in a dark room would also have temporarily blinded me. What I am "remembering" is an image my mind has reconstructed based on what I knew to be happening, and on the photograph we were able to take, which actually shows the moment the light bulb shattered.

The way in which we "see" the world is much more complex than many of us realize. It's easy to think of it as a straightforward process: our eyes take in information and send it to the brain, where it is recorded for later use. In reality, our brain is constantly working, constructing the world around us based on contextual cues, history, and the visual input we get from our eyes.

One of my favorite things about photography is how it allows us to play with the very concept of *seeing*. The camera is a more sophisticated and versatile "eye" than the eyes we humans are equipped with. The camera can move faster and record more precisely than we could ever hope to do, and this capacity makes it a tool that can fundamentally change our understanding of the world.

When the light bulb in my basement exploded, it didn't occur instantaneously. The hammer struck one side of the bulb; then cracks spread out from the impact point until the glass was too fractured to hold itself together. Kinetic energy from the impact forced those shards outward, and then gravity pulled them down. But it was only through the camera that my father and I were able to slow that moment down enough to see each of those individual motions—and turn them into memories.

The specific tool we used to slow down and isolate these movements was the camera's shutter speed. The shutter on

> The way in which we "see" the world is much more complex than many of us realize.

a camera is a barrier between the image plate or sensor and the light source, whether that is natural light or the camera's flash. The term *shutter speed* simply refers to how long you keep that barrier open and allow light to touch the image plate. It is one of the settings, along with aperture, that determines what the exposure of the shot will be, and different shutter speeds are used for different purposes.

Long-exposure photography, which we've talked about before, requires a very slow shutter speed: in some cases, a photographer might leave his or her shutter open for hours. Usually, someone would do this to photograph a very slow-moving object, like a star or planet, and the final photograph might be characterized by a bit of motion blur—that familiar line of light that traces the trajectory of an object across the frame. (Often, this is a way to make a shot appear dynamic and suggest that the objects in the frame are moving very fast.) A slow shutter speed is also great for shooting in low light because it gives the image plate more time to collect more of the available light, and that often reveals details that we wouldn't have seen in real life.

To photograph our smashed light bulb, my father and I used a fast shutter speed. By opening and closing the shutter in the smallest fraction of a second, we can freeze moments too brief to be seen in any other way. What my father and I did with the light bulb was technically a little bit different; with the shutter open the whole time, we simply darkened the room so that the flash provided the only light. By timing the flash to go off at the instant the light bulb shattered, we ensured that only that moment would be recorded on the image plate. Edgerton, the experiment's originator, invented an early version of strobe lighting to get his incredible motion-freezing shots; for some photographs, he used exposure times in thousandths of a second. In October 1987, *National Geographic* magazine famously dubbed him "The Man Who Made Time Stand Still."

A lot of business advice is about moving fast, growing exponentially, and making sure you don't miss opportunities. But I think there's a lot to be said for slowing things down every once in a while, or even for doing as Edgerton did and finding the beauty in a frozen moment. What would you be able to see if you could freeze the world? What details would emerge? How would your understanding of the world change?

When you adjust your shutter speed, the first thing you have to figure out is what kind of timescale you are working with. For example, if you want a clear photograph of a hummingbird in flight, you are talking about freezing movements that occur in tiny fractions of a second. On the other hand, if you want to track the moon's progress across the night sky, that process might take eight to ten hours. So what is your timeline?

I first began to seriously consider this when I went through Dan's Sullivan's Strategic Coach workshop and started thinking about how long I expected to live. Dan encouraged us to think beyond the current limitations of medical science and be expansive in our predictions. If medicine advances in the ways we can reasonably expect it to, if you are able to integrate healthy habits into your life, and if you live a low-risk lifestyle, how long will you live? I decided that my number is 120.

People often laugh when they hear that, but it gives me a longer timeline to work with—and a longer timeline is a slower one as well. I am fifty years old now, and being able to see myself as not yet middle-aged changes much about my approach to work and to life.

We live in a fast-paced world, and professionally, I can appreciate that. Photos in a Minute works because people want to have things instantaneously. But being in a constant rush can warp your perspective as well. A hummingbird's wings aren't really just a blur of movement. What we see in "real time" is the result of hundreds of clearly delineated up-and-down motions, but it's impossible to really know that unless we pause to look closer.

> A lot of business advice is about moving fast...but I think there's a lot to be said for slowing things down.

Visualizing life on a 120-year scale lets me see my goals not as huge monoliths, but as individual steps and movements. It doesn't just change my personal timeline; it also changes how I measure success. I am not chasing growth for its own sake; instead, I am measuring my progress by how I am moving through the discrete parts of the plan I have developed.

It wasn't always this way. When I was driven by more general imperatives like "growth!" or "more income!" I spent a lot of time jumping from one thing to the next. Without a plan, I tended to lose faith in things when they became difficult. Because I couldn't see the immediate challenge before me as part of a larger whole, I grew discouraged when it appeared that whatever I was attempting wasn't getting me any closer to the nebulous "more" that I needed. I also confused things that made me *feel* like I was progressing, with things that actually grew the business. Starting something new is always exciting, but it isn't always the best way to move toward a goal; in fact, starting a new project only divides your focus and lengthens the overall time the original project takes.

Chasing an undifferentiated conception of growth or progress also created frustrating and potentially destructive situations when I actually outgrew my capacity—or the company's capacity—to successfully manage all the tasks that had to get done. This is a problem that a lot of professionals face, especially creatives, because without clear plans broken down into small segments, it's very easy for things to get too complex too fast. Most creatives are very good at one particular thing and not so practiced at the dozens of other skills that a large, diverse business requires. If you aren't paying attention, you can easily find yourself in the position of needing to be an accountant, an HR manager, a marketing expert, and a logistics maven instead of whatever specific job you set out to do.

Often, it's hard to tell if things are getting too complex before it's too late and we've already become overwhelmed. Many entrepreneurs—including me, at one time—see themselves as "rugged individualists." We are independent types, and we often build our businesses from the ground up with few, if any, team members. We know, in the abstract, that we will eventually have to branch out and build a team to manage a larger-scale enterprise, but when you are living in the moment and handling problems as they arise, it's very hard to see that tipping point approaching.

Eventually, though, you will reach a point where things begin to fall apart. No matter how skilled you are or how hard you work, you are going to run up against the limitations of your abilities and the simple human constraints of finite time and energy. When you do arrive at that point and aren't prepared, it can be disastrous. For some people, it can wreck their mental and/or physical health. For others, it can implode their business. For me, at one point, it led to a mini retirement.

I was first introduced to the idea of mini retirements in the Tim Ferriss book *The 4-Hour Workweek*. The idea, essentially, is that high-powered CEOs and other business leaders will periodically take time off, completely leaving the corporate environment. They go away and do something else—anything else—for maybe six months, and when they come back, the extended time away will have jump-started their creative energy. The idea is based on the simple recognition that if we keep beating our head against the same wall over and over again, all we will do is sap our strength and erode our energy. Taking time to pause, regroup, and rethink allows us to solve problems in a different way.

My first attempt at a mini retirement was a result of my simply having become overwhelmed by the complexity of my business. I felt that I could no longer see clearly, so I had to stop everything to get a good look at the situation. I was essentially changing my shutter speed to adjust for a new situation. What had worked when I was building up the business was now inhibiting me now that I was in a different stage of career development. It was as though I'd tried to go from taking long-exposure shots of the moon to photographing birds in flight; if I didn't take a minute to change my settings, I'd only get a useless blur.

That first mini retirement was an incredible boon to me. Slowing things down allowed me to pinpoint the parts of my business that weren't working, and I was finally able to develop an actual growth strategy. I had just started getting into Strategic Coach at the time, so I incorporated my new sense of scale and vision for the future. I actually sat down and projected my growth in detail: how many locations I would be operating in, how many worldwide events I would be booking, and how many team members I would need. From there, things began to fall into place. When I could clearly see what my future looked like, I could prepare for it instead of struggling to catch up to situations that seemed to pop up out of nowhere.

I actually had a moment of deep appreciation and satisfaction recently when I sat down with my team to prepare for our busy season. As I was explaining how we would allocate our resources and handle the commitments we'd made, I realized something important: I was completely confident in what I was saying. I wasn't simply saying we could do these things because I knew we had signed contracts and *had* to do them; I knew we could do these things because I had put structures in place to get them done. I knew my travel team was going to make sure that my equipment and materials made it to each location. I knew my payroll professionals were going to get everyone invoiced and compensated on time. I knew that I could do the creative work in front of me, and I knew that we were all going to work together with a clear goal of having our biggest holiday season ever.

All of that preparation and certainty was a result not just of planning, but also of giving myself the time and space to plan. If I'd never stepped back from work, I could never have entered that more analytical mode; I would have been stuck in a purely reactive position instead of assuming a proactive one.

These days, I embrace what I now call "Free Days," and I do my best to get completely out of the work headspace when I take them. I am fortunate to have the ability to take a Free Day, because I know that those breaks are integral to my success.

I'm not idle during that time, however. I spend each break pursuing some sort of hobby or interest. During one break, I got really interested in homemade ice cream. I studied the process and conducted countless experiments of my own until I managed to produce some pretty tasty varieties (if I do say so myself). I liked one flavor well enough that I designed and printed my own logo and made labels. I gave it away to friends and acquaintances, who naturally assumed that I was making a pivot into the ice cream business. In reality, I wasn't doing anything of the sort; I was just letting my mind go where it wanted. I was allowing myself to focus intently on something completely different from my work in my photography company (which is mostly office time nowadays). It was sort of like switching from arm day to leg day at the gym: I was still exercising, but I was using different muscles, and the change of pace made me more well rounded.

Even after these breaks were over, I kept up with some of the new hobbies I'd developed, and I found it was good for me to have something to chew over in my mind that wasn't directly work related. I got really into beekeeping, and I eventually realized that going home and watching YouTube tutorials about raising honey bees was now occupying the space in my life that drinking used to inhabit. Instead of numbing my mind into silence, I was embracing my natural tendency to follow rabbit holes and become intensely interested in things. I found that when I let myself off the leash in that way, I could come back to work with a renewed sense of focus.

Before, my love of novelty and lack of planning was hurting me in business. I would get frustrated with a problem and try to launch some new project just to get that positive boost that comes from starting something. Now that I've compartmentalized my need for novelty and learned to satisfy it with nonwork stuff, I can approach my actual career more analytically.

When you are in the midst of something as vital and personal as building your business, you aren't necessarily seeing clearly. There's a lot of emotion bound up in our careers—anxiety about money, fear of failure, indecision about striking out on our own, a desire to succeed for our own self-esteem—and most of it isn't helpful when it comes to making practical decisions. Having the ability to pause, to slow down, and even to step away for a little while is absolutely critical. If you are making all your choices in the middle of a flurry of activity, seeing no further than the immediate work in front of you, all you are really doing is making your best (and often emotionally fraught) guess as to the right thing to do. And as we so often see in failed businesses, that kind of guessing is frequently wrong.

> We have to slow things down to see each action and reaction.

Instead, we have to slow things down—sometimes down to fractions of moments and fractions of movements—to see each action and reaction, each instance of cause and effect.

CHAPTER 6

– Depth of Field –
The Horizon Is a Vista,
Not an End Point

When we talk about an image's "depth of field," we are talking about how much of the image is in focus. For people who aren't very familiar with photography, that can seem like a weird idea. Shouldn't the *whole* picture be in focus? But "focus" in photographic terms isn't the same as "visible." We manipulate the focus of a shot—the area where the greatest detail is visible—to highlight and sharpen specific elements of the photo, usually the subject and its immediate surroundings.

Sometimes, the difference is extreme. If you are photographing a very small detail, like an insect or a single rose, you could adjust your settings so you have a very shallow depth of field. Only that one tiny object would be in sharp focus, while the world around it appears to be a blur of color. A deep depth of field, by contrast, might be used when you want to capture a sweeping vista. If you are photographing a mountain range, you could use a deeper depth of field to ensure that the grass in the meadows below is as clear and precise as the snow-capped peaks above.

One of the things that people often misunderstand about photography is that it isn't simply about recording reality (though that can definitely be part of it); it is visual communication. A photographer wants to tell you something with his or her pictures, and they will use all the tools at their disposal to communicate that message. Depth of field is a great way of telling the viewer what is important. By rendering the background less clear, we are able to draw the eye exactly where we want it, whether it's to a face, an object, or a piece of the landscape. To manipulate depth of field is to manipulate where the attention—and thus the mental energy—goes.

Applying the concept of depth of field to our lives and work really just means accepting a truth that we all know: you can't focus on all of the details all of the time. We don't have the visual acuity or the mental agility to see and understand every part of the picture before us at every turn. Inevitably, we are going to focus on some things and relegate others to the less clear "background."

The problem with this is that, all too often, it's a nearly unconscious process. Unlike a photographer carefully selecting the appropriate depth of field for the vision he or she has imagined, we pick areas of focus haphazardly, based on what we feel we should be doing rather than what will actually move us closer to our goals.

One big problem I've seen with a lot of entrepreneurs is a failure to modulate their depth of field. Some—the head-in-the-clouds, tinkerer types—go way too shallow and focus exclusively on some very granular detail of their business or product while overlooking the many other elements of their career. Much more common, however, is the reverse: entrepreneurs who deepen their depth of field to encompass all aspects of the project of starting a business. The trouble is, they can't sequence and prioritize all the things they need to do if everything appears to have the same importance.

I once appeared on Dan Sullivan's podcast, and we talked about this idea, which he likened to someone setting "the horizon" as his or her goal. The problem, of course, is that the horizon is a shifting target; it's impossible to actually "reach" the horizon, just as it's impossible to get away from one's shadow. Dan talked about people getting so caught up in their biggest goals that they became overwhelmed by all the day-to-day stuff that stretches between them and that tempting horizon. He calls this "getting lost in The Gap™."[1]

---

1 Scott Proposki, "How Entrepreneurial Advice Became Lifesaving Wisdom," interview by Dan Sullivan, https://resources.strategiccoach. com/audios-and-podcasts/how-entrepreneurial-advice-became-life-saving-wisdom-with-guest-scott-proposki.

I see this problem as a fundamental failure to adjust one's depth of field. If the horizon is ultra clear and your immediate surroundings are a blur, that's a recipe for failure in the moment. I, myself, got an object lesson in this problem a few months before I appeared on Dan's podcast.

It was early spring in New Hampshire, and I had decided to go on a hike with my faithful dog, Chip, a beautiful chocolate Labrador retriever. It was a challenging hike, but not more challenging than others I'd done before, and the terrain on the way up was relatively clear, so I didn't bother to bring my snowshoes. Halfway through the hike it began to snow, lightly but steadily. By the time I reached the summit there was a good amount of snow on the ground, but it wasn't more than I figured I could handle. However, there were some variables I'd forgotten to account for in my decision-making process.

The route down from the summit—my intended route home—was shielded from the sun by the mountain itself, which meant it was much colder on that side. Plus, all the snow that had fallen in recent weeks, and then that afternoon, had been able to pile up there undisturbed and unmelted. I couldn't tell just from looking at it how deep it was—or might become—but I assumed that since the weather had been mild recently, there couldn't be that much snow. That was my first major mistake.

> The concept of depth of field means you can't focus on all of the details all of the time.

My second was deciding to keep going down the other side of the mountain, sticking to my intended route. In retrospect, I should have turned around and retraced my steps. But that would have been a longer trip (at least in terms of miles on the map), and it was getting a little closer to dark than I would have liked. Plus, I've always been the kind to press ahead once I've picked a path. It's a trait that has definitely served me well in business, where being able to forge ahead is often rewarded, but it also has some big downsides. Forging ahead on a bad path just makes the journey longer and more difficult—as I was about to discover.

By the time I'd gotten part of the way down from the summit, I knew I had a problem. There was much more snow than I'd imagined there would be, and with every step I was sinking deeper and deeper. My dog, Chip, was virtually buried and had to keep leaping up to gain any ground at all. My hiking boots filled with snow, and my progress was slow.

By the time I recognized that I'd made a mistake, trying to go back the way I'd come was no longer an option. I'd be fighting the same snowdrifts, only now I'd be going uphill, and it was late enough by then that it would be pitch black by the time I made it back up to the summit (assuming I made it back up there at all), and I really didn't feel equipped to fumble my way down a mountain in the dark. From where I was now, it was only three miles back to the trailhead along my chosen path. Three miles at the summit had seemed like no big deal, but when I found myself struggling through four-to-six-foot snowdrifts, it began to feel impossible.

All the dangers of the situation seemed to hit me at once: I hadn't told anyone specifically where I was going, and while my wife would surely notice if I didn't come back, it might take her hours or days to figure out where to look for me. The nights were also more than cold enough to cause hypothermia, and I had dressed for a moderate afternoon hike in the sunshine. I also hadn't brought more than a few hours' worth of water. I wasn't at all prepared for a night in the wilderness.

Despite being in snow nearly up to my hips, I was actually sweating as I paused to look at the sinking sun on the white horizon. I thought about all the bad potential outcomes I was facing now. I looked out at the vast, white surface before me, featureless except for the occasional tree sticking out of the snow, and I thought about how three miles might as well be the distance from here to Mars.

Then, as I stared at that hopeless horizon, I had another thought: The Gap—Dan Sullivan's concept, the gap between where you are and where you want to be. I'd gotten caught in it in a very literal way. It would have been funny if I hadn't been so worried about frostbite!

I knew that in order to get out of this literal "gap," I was going to have to change my thinking. I had to adjust my area of focus; my current depth of field was far, far too deep. I was looking at the whole journey and preemptively defeating myself in my head. Instead, I had to adopt a very shallow depth of field; I had to find one small element of this task and focus on it without bringing in all the larger concerns.

I picked a large boulder that I knew from previous hikes was about a mile from my current location. I visualized the boulder as clearly as I could, and I set it not only as a goal, but also as my *only* goal. I wasn't going to think about the snow or the time or the exhaustion; I was only going to think about that boulder. I made it so large and prominent in my mind that everything else receded into the faintest blur.

Get to the boulder! Get to the boulder! I repeated that mantra to myself as I pushed through the snow. And when I got to that boulder, I paused to catch my breath . . . but I didn't let myself expand my focus again. Instead, I picked a new detail—a trailhead sign I knew was about two-thirds of a mile away—and did the same thing again. I absolutely refused to expand my thinking further than those specific milestones, because I knew if I did, I was going to start thinking about what-ifs, and those questions would only bring fear with them. Fear breeds panic, and once you panic, you give up all control over a situation.

I got down the mountain in that way, picking one milestone after another until finally, gratefully, I saw my truck in its parking spot at the trailhead. It was twilight by the time I got there, probably only ten or fifteen minutes from full dark, and I was cold, wet, and tired . . . but Chip and I were both safe and unharmed.

Entrepreneurs, like mountain climbers, are often encouraged to "think big," but it is often our ability to adjust our thinking to focus on incremental details that saves us. Adjustment is key here, because neither mode of thinking is the solution to every situation. It's just as important for us to be able to imagine expansive futures as to fine-tune small details, and an inability to shift our gears in that way leaves us open to a lot of avoidable problems.

With ADHD, I find myself toggling between these two ways of thinking pretty naturally. From spending hours tinkering with settings to get the perfect shot to my elaborate dreams of professional expansion, my mental depth of field fluctuates constantly. It's only relatively recently that I've been able to recognize what is happening in those moments and take control of that process. Being able to make these adjustments is only one piece of the puzzle; we also have to learn, as a photographer does, to assess the scene and make correct judgments about what adjustments are needed.

A few years ago, I was intensely focused on one particular customer. This was potentially a very big account—the kind that could change the way I did business in terms of reach and visibility. I was very close to making a deal with this client, and finalizing that process occupied almost all of my mental energy at the time—or, at least, that's what I thought. In reality, I was operating with a very deep depth of field, thinking far ahead to what I could do once this client signed on the dotted line, and how it would change things for my business. I wasn't actually looking at the moving parts of the deal still in progress—and while I was busy with the big picture, the deal was stalling out.

> We are encouraged to "think big," but our ability to adjust our thinking to focus on incremental details is critical.

At first, I couldn't figure out what was going on. We'd had several very positive meetings, and everything they'd said led me to believe they were as eager to work with me as I was to work with them. Yet, after I gave them the contract to sign, there was radio silence.

Around this time, I was on a flight back to Boston from Toronto, and during my flight I popped open my Microsoft Surface Book and opened every email and document tied to this deal. I kept coming back to one question: Why? Why would this previously responsive and enthusiastic customer ghost me right now? I turned it over and over in my mind until it occurred to me: it had to be something about the contract.

The contract was the only new element of our relationship, and as soon as I'd introduced it, the client had disappeared. So I dug out my copy of the contract and started going through it line by line. The legal language was one of those details I hadn't thought much about previously. I was no lawyer, obviously, and so I recognized early on that I would need to delegate that part of the business to someone with specialized expertise. We'd hired one of the biggest law

> We have to learn to make correct judgments about what adjustments are needed.

firms in Boston to write all of our contracts, so I simply assumed that everything there was industry standard. As I actually looked through the contract, though, I saw that it was much more one-sided than I had realized.

I would never sign this, I thought. It was all very confrontational, and set up an adversarial relationship between the customer and my company. My conversation with Dan over lunch that day was ringing in my ears; he had said, "Our eyes only see and our ears only hear what our brains are looking for."

The next morning I jumped out of bed and rushed to brew my favorite coffee to wash down my first dose of Adderall, and then sequestered myself in my office for a full Focus Day. I personally rewrote the contract to bring it more into line with what I had assumed we were offering all along. Additionally, I crafted an email explaining the situation and assuring the client that the other documents did not reflect how we viewed our working relationship with them.

Three days later, I had a signed PDF copy of the agreement in my inbox, and since then, our growth has been shaped, in many ways, by our relationship with that one client. My law team, of course, was just doing the job I'd hired them to do—protecting me!

Being able to toggle between the fine print and the big themes is about more than just survival; it's also about how we want to experience our lives. I once took an aerial photo of a lighthouse on the coast of Maine, the famous Portland Head Light. The view from four hundred feet was breathtaking, and that image would be an important part of any complete depiction of that stretch of Maine's coastline. But a photograph of a minuscule crab struggling to surmount a few grains of sand is also part of the essence of that region. And even with a very deep depth of field, you can't see that crab's journey while you're looking at the shoreline. Each way of seeing privileges different parts of a whole, and it's only by shifting between them that we can get a total picture.

We live in a world where "more" and "faster" are watch-words, and it's easy to lose track of our immediate reality while in pursuit of our goals. I know this firsthand from times when my wife has had to remind me to step away from my iPhone at dinner, and from the many photo shoots on which I've been so busy thinking about the job in the larger context of the project, that I've had to take a moment to remember I was already *there*. In those moments, being able to recalibrate allows me to have a better experience. If I couldn't expand my thinking beyond each micro crisis of my business, I would miss the opportunity to really engage with what I already had—like the dinner with my wife that was already in front of me. The first rule of managing your settings, whether on a camera or in your life, is to determine not what you are seeing, but what you *want* to see. As you work through a task or move toward a goal, periodically take a break to consider the following: What am I looking at? And because of what I'm looking at, what am I failing to see?

> Take a break to consider: What am I looking at? Because of what I'm looking at, what am I failing to see?

CHAPTER 7

– Metering –
How Do You Choose
Your Team Members?

In the last couple of chapters, we've talked a fair bit about managing our time and being able to allocate our energy properly, but I want to discuss exactly how we can do that on a practical level. When you are launching your own business—or trying to maintain it—the idea of taking a moment to slow things down can seem laughable. If you stop, even for a moment, bills don't get paid, work doesn't get done, and none of the dozens of daily little emergencies that crop up in any small business get resolved.

"Superman Syndrome" is pretty common among people who are attempting to start their own businesses. We either *want* to do everything ourselves, or we feel we *have* to. At first, that's a pretty useful impulse; a one-person show can be more agile and effective with less overhead. It becomes a problem, however, when your business grows beyond the capability of just one person but your thinking does not. Delegating responsibilities isn't just a good idea; it's a skill, and one that many entrepreneurs have let atrophy after years of going it alone.

Letting go of that "rugged individualist" mind-set can be challenging because it requires you to be vulnerable in a new way. But when you are doing everything on your own and trying to wear all the hats in a business, you are putting yourself at risk. You may stretch yourself too thin, you may come up against an element of the business that you don't fully understand, and you may lose out on opportunities because you quite literally can't be in two places at once. As a one-person operation, your personal vulnerabilities are your *professional* vulnerabilities . . . but for the most part, these are risks that you know and understand. So if you know you have trouble keeping track of paperwork or that you often overcommit yourself, you have a lifetime of managing those tendencies to prepare you for the fallout that results from making that same kind of mistake in a professional setting.

When you start to expand your business, however, and you begin to give meaningful responsibilities to other people, suddenly your risks are a lot more mysterious. Is this new person going to be inappropriate with a customer or bungle a job? Are they going to quit abruptly or steal from you? Bringing in a new person means bringing in their unknown flaws, and for someone who has nurtured a business from the ground up, that can be scary.

So how can we build a team that is effective and appropriate for the work at hand without feeling like we've handed our baby off to a stranger? The key is proper metering.

Metering is the act of measuring how much light is on a scene and determining exactly where that light is falling, and this information is crucial for selecting aperture and shutter-speed settings for the proper exposure. Back in the day, it used to be done with a handheld light meter, but most cameras these days have built-in meters. In fact, with today's cameras, you can even select different meter modes that automatically adjust the settings to highlight different elements of the image. Handheld light meters still exist, however, and they are generally more sensitive and precise than the integrated variety. If you're working on a complex scene with uneven lighting, an external light meter is the tool you need.

> Delegating responsibilities isn't just a good idea; it's a skill.

Metering was once one of the foundational steps in the process of taking a photograph. It was a bit like measuring twice before cutting a piece of wood—a way of gathering critical information that would affect how you approached the work you were going to do. Essentially, it saved the photographer the tedious job of taking lots and lots of photos with different settings as he or she tried to guesstimate the optimum exposure for the scene. Of course, this was also when photographers were using film, and would have to go home and develop all those pictures to select the one that worked. Now, when we can snap a hundred photos in a minute or two and immediately judge the results, many people no longer feel the need to do as much prep work.

I like metering though. I prefer going into a shoot with a plan, and I appreciate having as much information as possible; I think it's important to take the measure of a scene before I start working with it.

I approach team building in a similar way: I want to gather all the relevant information before I make any decisions. When it comes to human beings, metering is about pinpointing strengths and weaknesses. Just as a scene has some areas that are brighter and others that are darker, each individual brings something unique to the table even though he or she may fall short in other ways. I don't necessarily place a value judgment on these traits, just as I don't necessarily think that a darker area of a scene is "worse" than a brighter one; it just has to be managed differently with the proper settings.

In terms of a workplace environment, that management usually takes the form of teams within teams. I look for people who fit well with my existing personnel—not necessarily because they are similar, but because the ways in which

they are different are comple-
mentary. If I have someone who
is extremely creative and excellent
at generating new ideas, but who
struggles with logistical issues and
scalability, I would pair him or her
with a more pragmatic thinker who

> When it comes to humans, metering is about pinpointing strengths and weaknesses.

may not have artistic ideas to share, but who instantly knows
how to translate others' ideas into workable plans.

This approach is part of why I always use the language of
"teams," "teamwork," and "team members" rather than "staff"
and "employees." I don't see myself as "the boss." I tell every
new team member I am not the boss; I'm the coach, and we
have a team, and we will win this game together. I see my
company as a unit that is working toward a common goal,
and each person is a piece of the whole. It's not just about
having extra hands to help with work; it's about strategizing
and selecting the right individual for each role. I'm not
hiring "worker number three"; I'm finding my point guard
or safecracker—a specialized person for a specialized role.

Unfortunately, getting the right people to fill those
roles is a lot easier said than done. The traditional interview
process only offers us the narrowest view of a person; it's
a snapshot, rather than a full photo shoot. To get a fuller
sense of someone and make an informed assessment, you
really need to gauge his or her various qualities. Different
people might use different tools to do this. Some people

find the interview process sufficient, whereas others like to have applicants fill out unorthodox questionnaires, or bring people in for "active" interviews that involve navigating typical problems they would face on the job. Still others simply trust their instincts, and some use staffing services or recruiters who do the legwork for them.

My company has adopted a system that I first encountered at my coaching workshop at Strategic Coach, a personal-assessment tool called the Kolbe Index.[2] There are several variations of the Kolbe Index; the one I took, the A Index, is a bit like a personality test. It tells you what your natural strengths and weaknesses are in the workplace, and how to make the most of those strengths for yourself and your business. Instead of sorting people into general types, as the Myers–Briggs Type Indicator does, the Kolbe Index shows you how intensely you evince certain traits, and offers an assessment of how those traits might work together to enable you to create a balanced team within your organization, with each person's strengths and weaknesses accounted for. The idea is to measure not who you are so much as how you do things. I have found that knowledge incredibly helpful, both personally and professionally.

The Kolbe A Index grades you on your ability to strategize and gather information (they call this "Fact Finder"), your ability to execute a plan ("Follow Thru"), your tolerance

2 http://www.kolbe.com

for risk and ability to take action ("Quick Start"), and finally, your problem-solving skills ("Implementor"). You receive a number from 1 through 10 for each skill, with 1 meaning you have a very low ability to master that skill set, and 10 meaning you are highly proficient at it.

My results were, in many ways, not surprising. I got a 9 in "Quick Start ," but my "Follow Thru" score was very low—as any of my teachers in high school probably could have predicted.

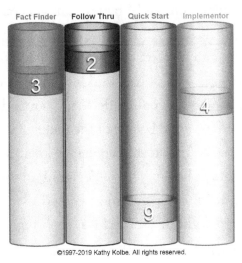

Seeing it all laid out on paper was valuable, however. It took things that I "knew" on some abstract level and put them together like a puzzle—or rather, like *part* of a puzzle. Looking at my results, it was very easy to see where I would benefit from some outside help. I needed someone to balance me, a person with a high Follow Thru score to complement my "forge ahead" instincts.

Again, this was something I might have known on some level—that I need a detail-oriented person to be able to keep a project moving after the initial rush has faded—but I didn't know how to find that in someone else, especially a relative stranger. I didn't know what questions to ask them or how to tell from a short conversation what they would be bringing to the professional environment—or rather, I didn't know how to figure those things out *in any definitive way*. I relied fairly often on how I felt about a person, or the "vibe" I got from our interaction, and I believe I'm generally a pretty good judge of character. But seeing the "stats" on a person is illuminating, and it offers another layer of confidence that I just didn't have when I was working exclusively from my own hunches about people. I decided then and there that the Kolbe Index would be one of the meters I would use to evaluate potential new team members. I knew it would give me actual data to help me make decisions, in the same way that a light meter would give me a numerical measurement of the ambient light in a scene I was shooting.

The Kolbe Index may not be for everyone, but for me, it's been invaluable. In general, I think it's very important that we have something other than just our feelings or instincts to guide us when it comes to expanding our teams. Our instincts, like our eyes, are easily fooled, especially when we don't have much time to spend with a subject. That's why we invent objective tools—so we don't have to rely exclusively on our fallible human perceptions.

Shortly after I started using the Kolbe Index, I was presented with an opportunity to see just how far off the mark my instincts could actually be. I was in the process of hiring someone for a critical position at the company. The person I was hiring would have a lot of responsibility and independence, and I'd spent a long time looking for the right candidate. She was, I believed, highly skilled and professional. She had impressed me as capable and on the ball—the sort of person with a high Follow Thru score, I'd imagined. I felt good about my decision. So good, in fact, that it didn't even occur to me that I hadn't asked her to take the Kolbe Index assessment until my own coach asked me about it.

I considered it almost a formality at that point, but I was curious to see what her results would be, so I sent her the test and asked her to take it before we proceeded with the hiring. A few days went by, then a week. Then another week.

Hmm, I thought, *probably not a 9 on Follow Thru, then.* I was a little surprised by this development, because it didn't match what I'd seen of her in interviews, but this wasn't by any means a deal breaker. She could have gotten busy or had an emergency or any number of other things, so I still considered her my top candidate for the job. However, I was now more curious than ever to see how she scored on the assessment, so I sent her a gentle email prompt about it.

It took her almost three more weeks to complete the test, and when the results were sent to me, I was baffled. It said her test was "incomplete," which I didn't even realize was possible. The test is online, and I didn't think it allowed you to move forward to the assessment page unless you'd answered all the questions. Thinking that something must have gone wrong with the results and perhaps I was reading it wrong, I called Kolbe's customer service team. They explained to me that my prospective employee's result was probably due to a major change in her life; perhaps she was unclear about what was next for her. I would better describe this by saying that her lens was out of focus and she didn't have the ability to focus on the next subject.

Nevertheless, I was still willing to work with her. I logged in to see her Kolbe report, and the results were eye-opening: "Your result indicates that you may not be currently getting the freedom to solve problems by using your natural instincts. You have conative strengths that give you a natural MO (Mode of Operation) that is being clouded temporarily. We refer to such situations as a period of *Transition*. During this time, you are probably experiencing an internal tug-of-war over the way you try to get things done. You may be trying to do whatever you believe you have to do to satisfy your present situation or the requirements of others."

At this point, it was almost like reading a mystery novel. The twists! The turns! I hadn't committed to hiring this person, and now I wondered whether or not I was comfortable with moving forward. I looked back at my notes from the day we met; I had written that "she just moved to Boston" and was "thinking of moving to L.A." next. Her current job helped her with "other work," which was what she really wanted to do. It was clear to me that I hadn't been listening to her the day we met, and that this information precisely aligned with the Kolbe Index report. This made me think about all the people I had hired in the past. We needed a meter, and the Kolbe Index would be my meter moving forward.

Later, I kept coming back to how close I'd come to handing over a huge amount of responsibility to someone I would have hired on the spot in my past—a person who wasn't in alignment with the future goals of my company.

I never heard back from her again; she vanished. Looking back at my notes and at the Kolbe results, all the signs were there. What if we'd hired her and she had done her vanishing act in the middle of our busy season? I never did have a chance to speak with her after her Kolbe Index assessment, and I wish I had; maybe I could have helped her in some way.

I have wasted a lot of time and money in the past trying to fix people instead of matching my company with the right individuals before hiring them. Perhaps in this case Dan Sullivan's reminder to have my new team members take the Kolbe Index assessment had just saved me $40,000 or more. How much does it cost your business to invest in a new team member only to then see them leave? If we could match our businesses with the best people, then those people would stay, and our businesses would be more profitable.

I was unnerved by the idea that I could interview someone several times, check her references, consult her work, and get a good feeling about her, only for her to get a lower Follow Thru score than I did! I now always use the Kolbe Index to evaluate prospective team members. When I can outline a measurable trait I want from someone, and can actually filter for that trait, my hiring choice makes for a more cohesive and effective team. It's the difference between saying, "I need someone who can work in the office," and saying, "I want a good focus manager to keep the team organized." The second ability is something you can actually measure, and thus something you can use to narrow your field of candidates.

Because everyone's needs are different, we are all going to select the metering tools that best fit our individual circumstances. I would recommend finding something external, and this could mean anything from a group of advisors to help you evaluate interviewees to a trial period to enable you to observe someone's work. Whatever you choose, the goal is to get outside of your own head. Expanding your business is all about taking some of the burdens off yourself—and all of us, no matter how independent and competent, can admit that we don't always see the world with clear and perfect focus. Sometimes we just need a little help, and acknowledging that is key to team building. Your company probably started with just you and your dreams, but the expansion of your company has to start with your honest assessment of yourself and your needs.

Remember how I introduced the Kolbe Index by talking about how I first took the test myself? That's actually a critical part of the metering process: understanding what you are already working with before making any additions. The most sensitive and accurate light meter in the world can only be of limited help if you don't understand how your camera works.

The more I learn about myself and think analytically about my professional strengths and weaknesses, the better I am able to assess others and recognize in them areas of overlap or difference. Taking the Kolbe Index was, in a way, sort of like receiving my ADHD diagnosis; it allowed me to put a name and shape to something that previously been just a feeling. And, as with ADHD, having a context and framework for understanding my own instincts and behavior has really helped me connect with others.

> Expanding your business is all about taking some of the burdens off yourself.

I've often heard it said about people with ADHD that "it takes one to know one," and from what I understand, that's true of people with a lot of other developmental or learning differences. Even before I thought of myself as someone with ADHD, I definitely felt a sense of kinship with certain people. There was something oddly predictable about them, even if it was just that they were predictably unpredictable. The major change now is that I can understand these mind-sets, these limitations and strengths, as part of a set of known and understood tendencies, and

I'm better able to work with them. The information I get from Kolbe gives me a larger vocabulary and a wider range of predictable behaviors to use when I'm planning for the future. This is invaluable to me, not just because it helps me build cohesive teams that work together seamlessly, but also because it allows me to work with people like me, people who may not have thought they'd ever be able to thrive in a "traditional" work environment.

I think part of the reason I started my own business was that, like a lot of photographers and entrepreneurs I've known, I couldn't imagine myself succeeding in a typical career. Partially, it was a belief that a nine-to-five wouldn't hold my interest or allow me to do what I was best at, but some of it was also fear that working in that way would be a lot like going to school. I felt like I'd end up discouraged, wondering why it was so hard for me to do what seemed so "normal" for everyone else.

I was lucky to have my father as an example. While he did work for a larger corporation, his job was nontraditional in the sense that it offered more room for creativity. I learned early in my life that there was a way to make money that didn't involve cubicles or trade school. I know there are a lot of other people out there, however, who may not want to build their own business but also feel ill-equipped to succeed as part of a team. Too often this leads to loss on both sides: some industry misses out on the creative energy and unconventional problem-solving that these people can offer, while they, themselves, lose out on opportunities to excel professionally and build careers they enjoy.

The approach I have developed is designed to bring people together in a way that enhances their strengths and gives people the support they need to do good work that they can feel good about. I think it's a positive structure for almost anyone, but especially for people who find the average workplace too boring, too restrictive, or too demanding. We are not the average workplace, and my reward for this approach is the genuine cohesion I see when I work with my teams.

During the month of December, I travel around the country visiting our Santa Experience pop-up stores to make sure things are running smoothly. Many of these stores are managed by local teams, and these trips provide a great opportunity for me to see how certain combinations of people are working together. It's remarkable to me how much fun these people are having. When you eliminate interpersonal friction by consciously putting together a group of individuals who complement one another, it's amazing how everyone can just lock in and focus on their goal—in this case, creating holiday memories!

Recently I went to a brand-new location in Texas, and I was particularly impressed with the team there. The team members worked together like clockwork—divvying up tasks, identifying and resolving problems, and doing it all with a comradely vibe. I asked the team leader how long they'd been working together, and I was shocked when he told me, "Two days."

That team in Texas was the unanticipated ripple effect of a new team-building process I had implemented at the very top. The way I chose my most immediate point people and the goals I set for developing remote teams meant that, even when I wasn't personally overseeing the hiring or formation of a group, it was still organized with an eye toward a functional, effective whole. And that has made all the difference for the individuals on the ground. Their comfort and ease in the workplace enables them to provide better, more enthusiastic and responsive service for our customers.

Working in a creative industry *should* be enjoyable. It *should* be fulfilling. That doesn't mean it's not work, or that it's never challenging or frustrating, but working in a creative field enables us to feed the curious, artistic side of ourselves. I think many people don't even realize how much unnecessary anxiety and difficulty poor personnel management can add to what should be an enjoyable job. People want to do good work. They want to take pride in what they do and they want to work with people who are enjoyable and effective. I'm of the opinion that inherently "bad" employees are actually pretty rare . . . but poorly managed and resourced employees are unfortunately quite common.

In the end, expanding the scope of your company is about trust: It's about trusting that other people will be ready for the responsibilities you give them. It's about trusting that your company is ready for growth. It's about trusting yourself to make good decisions. Most of all, it's about trusting that other people will be able to share your goals and your vision. All of that will require a leap of faith, but knowledge, analytics, and tools that allow you to measure and strategize are ways of shrinking that leap until it's just one more step into the future.

> In the end, expanding the scope of your company is about trust.

CHAPTER 8

– ISO –

Eliminating the Noise

ISO is a measure of sensitivity. It indicates how much light it will take for an image to register on a camera's film or image sensor. Together, ISO, shutter speed, and aperture make up the "exposure triangle." The higher the ISO, the more sensitive the image plate, allowing you to shoot relatively clear images even in low-light conditions. As a general rule, however, it's best to shoot at a lower ISO if you can, because increasing the ISO also increases the noise in the resulting photograph.

Noise (also called "grain") is those tiny little specks, sometimes colorful, sometimes black and white, that can make images look blurry or dirty. If you've ever blown an image up to a very large size and been disappointed to find it was noticeably less clear, you've seen digital-image noise. It appears in high-ISO images (among others) because, well, it was there all along. The higher sensitivity of your ISO settings simply picks up more noise because it picks up more of the available light in general. You may have heard the term "signal to noise ratio," usually describing audio clarity, but the same principle works for photographs. A higher-quality image contains significantly more useful visual information than grainy noise.

It always struck me as a counterintuitive idea—that something could work better yet deliver a less desirable outcome. I've since embraced the concept, however, because I've realized something important: *more* is not the same as *better*.

You might think that's a pretty obvious conclusion, but you'd never know it from the way most people function day to day. We often take it for granted that if *some* is good, then *a lot* would be great, and we embrace excess often without really thinking about what it means to have an abundance of a good thing. This is definitely true in entrepreneurial culture, where everyone wants to grow and expand, and it's easy to forget that the more variables you add to a situation, the more complications you have to navigate. Sometimes, the complications can become so overwhelming that, like an image obscured by noise, you can no longer benefit from the extra "good stuff." In those moments, we have to be able to adjust a range of settings to dial back the noise and reveal the image we actually want to see.

Having ADHD sometimes feels like someone has turned up the ISO in my brain. I can't help but see everything, no matter how important or unimportant, and each element is just as prominent as any other. It means that the contract I need to review can seem just as urgent as the broken zipper on my camera bag, and every broken zipper or camera malfunction or paperwork error that crops up can push aside even genuinely pressing concerns the same ways dots of noisy color can blur the clean lines in a photograph.

Before medication, one of the best ways I found to turn down my mental ISO was to get on a plane. True, it's not the most convenient solution, but something about being in a metal tube flying high above the earth just . . . slowed everything down for me. The relative lack of stimulation on a plane helped me isolate one or two concerns and focus all my mental energy on working those things out. One day I would be photographing Sylvester Stallone in Los Angeles, and the next day I would take a red-eye flight to New York City to work on Bravo's reality show, *The Real Housewives of New York City*, or jet to another location to work on HBO's *The Sopranos*. I would use that time, sitting in a jet plane going five hundred miles an hour while my mind was going four hundred miles an hour, to try to master meditation in order to achieve mental clarity and emotional calm before I got home to resume my everyday life. I would arrive at Boston Logan International Airport as the sun was rising, and I would try to make it home to see my wife before she left for her job as a nurse. She would ask, "How was your trip?" Most times I would just answer, "It was good," and say nothing else! Expending the mental energy required to recap these experiences would cause me to lose focus, and I wanted to stay focused and turn my ISO noise down.

It was funny—I needed to be in a plane going five hundred miles an hour in order to slow my brain down a little. Later, with therapy and treatment—and changes to my schedule, like instituting Focus Days—I learned how to get the same effect without buying a cross-country plane ticket.

The first challenge in eliminating noise from our personal and professional lives is determining which concerns are distractions and which are valid and important. It's not always as easy as it may seem, and it all depends on your goals in a specific situation. Even what we could call visual "noise"—that grainy, thick quality in an image—can be used in some cases to create an effect the photographer wants. For example, if you want to make an image evoke a certain nostalgic visual mood, you might actually want more noise because it can mimic the look produced by earlier photographic methods.

One strategy is to take the time to notice the distractions around you. It works like this: You set yourself up in a comfortable and familiar environment, the kind of place in which you might normally work. Then, you sit down and record the distractions that occur around you. You will be amazed by the small details you never noticed before.

Maybe you don't consciously hear the weird hum the fridge makes or how the notifications popping up on your phone draw your eye, but when you actually sit down and record all these details, you will be surprised by how often they divert your attention.

The more you recognize and understand the distractions in your life, the better able you'll be to eliminate and avoid them. Maybe you need to put your phone in another room while you work. Perhaps you can't effectively get things done at a certain time of day. If you work from home, you might need to go to a coffee shop or an office so you aren't reminded of dishes piling up in the sink and other domestic tasks.

> The first challenge in to determine which concerns are distractions and which are valid.

For me, one of the most important things has been structuring my time in a deliberate way. When I know that I have specific Focus Days interspersed with "Free Days," it is easier to banish those errant urges to work on or think about whatever pops up in my head. I call it "squirrel syndrome," when one small flash of an idea—"I need to send out that sales deck from last week's sales meeting," for example—can send me off on a tangent, far from whatever my initial task was. When I devote structured time to specific work, it's easier for me to stop those tangents before they change my focus. Something as simple as being able to say, "Okay, I will write that proposal tomorrow during my focus time. This time is for my current project," helps immensely in terms of keeping myself on track.

Learning to identify noise versus signal in the moment has helped me develop a kind of distraction triage while I am working. It goes like this:

Step One: Identify my current goal. For example, I might need to complete a review of a contract and send it to the client before the end of the business day.

Step Two: Determine what is pulling my attention. Maybe someone is texting me about a potential new opportunity.

Step Three: Ask myself if addressing the distraction will help me accomplish my goal. In this case, it would not.

Step Four: Find a time when I can deal with the new concern. In this case, I would say to myself, "After EOB, you can read the texts and analyze the offer."

Once I've identified a bit of "noise" and carved out a time when I can deal with it, it's a lot easier to turn my attention back to my primary objective. It's not a perfect system, of course. Sometimes there are genuine emergencies that require you to shuffle priorities and, especially in my case, there are times when the interruptions come fast and furious. There are times when I have to go through this process with different distractions maybe a dozen times in an hour of work. It can be difficult to keep going through what feels like the same motions over and over again. Over time, I've gotten better and faster with this process; these days, it feels almost automatic. I can't toggle a switch in my brain that turns down the grain and brings the vital facts into focus, but having a step-by-step process and being aware of it is the next best thing. I was very glad I'd put so much effort into figuring out my system when, a few years ago, I faced the most high-stress test of my focus yet.

In 2016 I was hired as the official photographer for the White House Easter Egg Roll. For those who are not familiar with this event, it is a large Easter egg hunt hosted and attended by the president. Thousands of kids come from all over to participate, and, of course, the Easter Bunny is always in attendance. All in all, more than thirty thousand people were on the White House lawn that day, and it was my team's job to capture the most compelling, memorable moments.

The distractions on this job were unlike anything I'd ever encountered. I'd photographed famous people and big events, but nothing with the kind of security apparatus or historic cachet of the White House. There was also a lot of pressure—most of it self-imposed—to do my best work. This was the kind of opportunity that an event photographer dreams about, and I wanted to prove to myself and others that I could do top-level work.

In my experience, an anxious mind is a distracted mind. When I'm worried or nervous about something, I'll latch on to any little detail and hyperfocus on it like a dog mangling a chew toy. I knew when I took the job that I would need to be especially vigilant about maintaining focus. Not only were there a tremendous number of moving parts and a lot of people and space to cover, but I would also have to resist the urge to overthink details and dwell on small things that might go wrong.

Mentally, I began preparing for the project months in advance. Virtually as soon as we got the contract, I was going over my strategy for the day in my head—tweaking details, thinking about possibilities, and trying my best to inoculate myself against last-minute fears. I went over my plan—how I was going to deliver on my promise of "photos in a minute" for thousands of guests—again and again until I could have sleepwalked my way through it. What I was trying to do, and what I eventually did, was become so familiar with the plan that, when I thought about the event, the smooth execution of that plan was all I could see.

I visualized my strategy so often that when we actually started on the morning of the roll, and things began to happen as I'd scheduled, it felt like confirmation of my vision. It was almost like I could tell the future. I knew what would follow everything that was taking place in front of me, and the more things adhered to the plan, the more confident I became.

I was able to switch on autopilot, going through with a strategy that I'd practiced in my mind thousands of times before. Because I wasn't reacting in the moment, I didn't have to fend off a constant stream of worries. I knew *what* needed to happen, I knew *how* to make it happen, and I was watching it all unfold right in front of me. It was like watching a photo develop in the chemical bath and knowing exactly what you will see because you've already envisioned it perfectly in your mind's eye.

But while you can control a lot about a situation—your team, your approach, your equipment, your time management—you can't control everything. You especially can't control how other people are going to behave. Even the most comprehensive plan in the world can't always account for the eccentricities of human nature.

We were about midway through the program and my team and I had stepped back to evaluate how things were going, when the general tenor of the event started to change. It wasn't immediately obvious what was going on, but I think we all started to sense that something was different. While we were brainstorming some tweaks to our coverage of the Easter Egg Roll, I began to notice that the Secret Service agents suddenly seemed a whole lot more present. They had been there all along, of course, and in the days before the event, our whole team had been subject to interviews and inspections when we brought in our equipment. Before, however, they had seemed to melt into the background and kept out of the festivities themselves. Now, I could see a few agents moving through the crowd, and I looked up at one point to see additional agents on the roof of the White House.

I was just thinking, *"That seems weird,"* when a helicopter appeared over the White House lawn. Okay, that was definitely not normal Easter Egg Roll protocol. I told my team

> While you can control a lot about a situation, you can't control everything.

members to continue working the event, and excused myself to speak with a park ranger. (Technically, the front lawn of the White House is a national park and, like any other park, it is overseen by rangers.)

I asked the ranger what was going on, but he didn't have any details. Meanwhile, people were ushering their kids off the lawn; as I spoke to the ranger, I could actually see the crowd shrinking. I unlocked my phone to see if anyone had tried to call me, and saw a Twitter notification from CNN: there had been a shooting at the Capitol. I scanned the article quickly, but details were sparse. I was sure, though, that this had to be what was causing the heightened state of alert all around me.

It was a surreal contrast to the day before, when I had been on the same lawn, setting up and preparing to photograph the event. President Obama had walked right by me on his way to the tennis court, and the lawn had bustled with landscapers, rangers, visitors, and others. I knew that the Secret Service must have maintained a presence even then, but the feeling of the afternoon had been light and peaceful, with no sign that anyone was worried about anything. It was incredible how, in an instant, everything could change, and this elaborate infrastructure I hadn't really noticed could suddenly be at the forefront of all that was happening. It was a little like when something goes wrong in your car, and suddenly the dash lights up in a blaze of alerts. Who knew you even had a "low tire pressure" sign? But it was there all along, quietly monitoring the situation until something changed and it had to be activated. And, much like when all the lights blink on your dashboard, the change on the White House lawn seemed to create a low-level panic in everyone who noticed it.

I had a choice in that moment. I could have chased what certainly appeared to be a pretty urgent new concern. I could have glued myself to my phone, or found my official contacts and tried to get more information out of them. I could have let the uncertainty and apprehension of what was happening shape the rest of my experience at the White House.

Instead, I went through my questions:

What was my goal? Well, even though people were leaving the grounds early, no one had canceled the Easter Egg Roll, and it was still my job to photograph it.

What was pulling my focus? Fear that an armed person may be nearby.

Would addressing that new concern further my ultimate goal? And that was the tough one because you could argue that maintaining one's personal safety comes before all other concerns. But I decided that trawling Twitter for news or finding and bothering a Secret Service agent probably wouldn't make me any safer. I was in one of the most protected places in the world and I'd seen with my own eyes that actions were being taken to secure the scene. Plus,

President Obama and his family were still participating in the event. If violence were imminent, surely they would have been taken to safety already. I had to trust that the security personnel were doing their job, and, if they were, that meant there was nothing left for me to do but do mine as well.

Finally, I decided that, after all this was over, I'd catch up on everything that was happening because I could tell, even without Dad right there to remind me, that this was going to make for a great story someday.

With my decision made, I was able to put the helicopters, the Twitter alerts, and the Secret Service in the back of my mind. I dialed down all that noise and refocused on my plan for the event. My team and I got back to work and covered the rest of the Easter Egg Roll just as we'd planned. Being able to deliver pictures to smiling kids was a great reinforcement of my choice to focus on the work. My vision was being realized and it was only possible because I had been able to adjust my settings and correctly identify the most important parts of the picture.

As it turned out, the beefed-up security response at the White House was actually a result of two unrelated incidents. A man had brandished a gun at the Capitol Visitor Center before being shot and killed by officers on the scene while, at the White House, a woman had tried to remove a barrier and illegally enter the Easter Egg Roll. The two individuals had no connection, but the shooting had, understandably, raised the general level of readiness around the White House—thus the helicopters. I personally was never in any danger, and my instincts—that the White House security force would handle the situation and evacuate as needed—were correct.

In a way, what I saw that day on the White House lawn was an example of the kind of filtration that we all have to do to eliminate noise and isolate the useful information. Secret Service agents need to have a very high ISO setting; they need to be extremely sensitive to anything that might be a threat or even a precursor of a threat. That means that they have to take in a lot of information and evaluate it all with gravity and thoroughness. They have to "see" things like the woman attempting to trespass because, in their line of work, the difference between inconsequential noise and serious, important signals can be very slight. Still, their response showed that, although they have to consider all of this information seriously, they still have a sorting mechanism that helps them decide how to respond. After all, no one was hustled to an underground bunker or anything, and that was for the best. Being able to distinguish between distractions and important tasks and being able to respond accordingly account for the difference between a fun holiday celebration that thousands of people will remember for the rest of their lives and a ruined day for everyone.

In photography, we use a high ISO in situations where there is very little natural light because it helps us capture details that would otherwise go unnoticed. Like almost all of these camera settings we've discussed, there's no "good"

> We have to decide in our own lives how much noise is okay in the pursuit of our goals.

or "bad" ISO level; it all depends on the situation. Similarly, we have to decide in our own lives what constitutes noise and how much of it is okay in the pursuit of our goals. As always, your most important concern, your guiding light, should always be, "When all of this is said and done, what sort of picture do I want to see?"

CHAPTER 9

– Stabilization –
Keeping Your Balance

I've talked a lot in this book about focus—how to find it, how to maintain it, how to protect it from the daily onslaught of distractions we all face—but something I've touched on only briefly is the problem of focusing too much or too narrowly. I mentioned earlier that my tendencies toward hyperfocus (obsessing over the camera, fiddling with settings, tweaking photos) have generally been a positive in my life. Digging into those details has made me a better, more in-demand photographer and has definitely helped me professionally. But there's a downside to even positive hyperfocus. The nature of living requires us all to be multitaskers to some degree, and homing in too narrowly on one thing for too long can destabilize our entire lives.

Sure, there may be one or two eccentric geniuses out there who have the luxury of structuring their existence in such a way that they can just hole up in their laboratory and work out a problem for years, but almost everyone else has to juggle at least a few things. Dogs need to be walked, kids need to be fed, and spouses need to interact with you on occasion. The business of living doesn't disappear just because something more interesting is taking place. Major imbalances between work and life are so common for entrepreneurs and other self-employed people that it's basically accepted as "part of the deal" when you work for yourself. I've known some people to hyperfocus on a project so intensely that they forgo even basic things like showering and eating regularly.

In many ways, hyperfocusing on something "real" (meaning something that can plausibly be called "work") can mask the problem for longer than an obsession with Candy Crush Saga or painting miniatures might. During my most intense period of professional hyperfocus, I told myself it was okay that I spent almost no time with my family and friends, and worked at all hours, because it was *work*. Work is important, right? I was growing my business, so it was normal and even desirable that it should take up a huge chunk of my mental real estate.

What I didn't realize was that I had dangerously overloaded one part of my life and neglected the rest. The way I was allocating my personal resources wasn't sustainable, and in the long run, it would hurt my business as well as the rest of my life. I was rolling along like a car with three wheels; inertia was carrying me forward, but it couldn't stay that way forever. Unfortunately, I didn't see the crash coming until it literally almost killed me.

In 2003, my wife convinced me to take a vacation. When I say she "convinced" me, I don't mean she gave me a few brochures and we talked it over one night; she spent almost two years working on me, arguing that I needed some rest and time away from my phone, my computer, and all other distractions. Two years was what it took, because while I could see the wisdom in her suggestion, there was always some reason to say no. I had a big project, or I had to prepare for a *different* project, or we were starting an expansion, or we had to hire a new team member. Basically, I wasn't prioritizing any of the things my wife was talking about— maintaining interpersonal ties, refreshing myself, putting some distance between myself and work for a while—so business was always going to trump personal stuff, no matter how sensible or important it might be.

> Hyperfocusing on something "real" (meaning something that can plausibly be called "work") can mask the problem for longer.

I also kept avoiding a big vacation because every time my wife managed to get me to go away somewhere for even a day or two, I would immediately get a nasty cold that I would have to deal with for the next two weeks. I realize now that this probably happened because I was pushing myself so hard and treating my body so roughly that the moment I let my guard down, my immune system just collapsed. My body was trying to tell me to slow down and take a rest, but I wasn't listening to myself any more than I listened to my wife.

Finally, though, she talked me into it. She did all the legwork, finding and booking a Mexican cruise with several stops at beautiful beaches and other tourist attractions. It would be sunny and hot and all-inclusive; we wouldn't have to worry about meals, flights, or itineraries. Her real stroke of genius, though, was pointing out that I could use the trip as an opportunity to test out a new waterproof camera case I'd gotten for a project for the National Geographic Society. Of course, the idea of being able to tinker with a new toy clinched the deal, and I finally agreed to take the trip.

Almost as soon as we left, I caught my customary vacation cold. Fortunately, I was able to rest in our cabin, and it took a few days to get to our destination anyway, so I was less concerned about "wasting" the vacation time. By the time we arrived at the first of our scheduled stops, I felt well enough to hit the beach with everyone else. Lying on a beach chair under the blazing sun and watching everyone around me swimming and playing and having so much fun, I began to feel for the first time in a long time that there might be something to this whole "vacation" thing. Today I would call this sort of experience a "Free Day," and I understand how vital they are in terms of keeping me balanced and on track. At the time, though, I just figured that it was the beach atmosphere that was making the difference.

I even agreed to go snorkeling with a few other people (though I still insisted on bringing my newly waterproofed camera to try out). I hadn't really done much snorkeling before, but it seemed pretty easy, and focusing on someone else telling me what to do was not my strongest skill, so I quickly peeled off from the group. The water was perfect—that Crayola blue that you only see on TV—and full of multicolored fish and strange coral formations. And I was experiencing all of it through the lens of my camera.

With the benefit of hindsight, I can see now how I was using my camera as a way of filtering distractions. I knew that, in neutral circumstances, I would be overwhelmed by stimulation from the world around me. My ISO settings were sky-high in the days before medication, and I didn't know a lot of good ways to turn them down. Too much information and stuff to keep track of would make me feel overwhelmed and miserable and ruin the vacation. But if I could focus on the camera, if I could invest myself fully in the small details of a new photography challenge, I could soften some of the noise of the world and just enjoy myself. It was a strategy I'd been using since I'd first started photographing family gatherings as a kid, and it hadn't failed me yet.

What I hadn't really thought about, however, was how different the situation in which I currently found myself was from what I normally experienced. Fixating on my camera naturally meant paying less attention to my surroundings; in fact, that was exactly what I was trying to do. But there was an added layer of difficulty, and even risk, in ignoring the world around me when I was floating in the ocean versus sitting at a desk. At home, I'd go into my photography fugue and maybe forget some appointments or lose track of a conversation. Here, my lack of situational awareness put me in real danger.

And that's exactly what happened when I failed to notice some nearby Jet Skiers. To be clear, I did actually notice them, but I attached no importance to their presence. After all, I didn't need to take pictures of Jet Skis. If I had been paying attention, I might have realized that the wakes they were producing were going to hit me and could potentially swamp my snorkel, and, if I'd realized that, I could have surfaced or moved or otherwise avoided that obvious problem. Instead, I was taken completely by surprise when I got a lungful of seawater.

I still hadn't completely kicked my cold, and the sudden saltwater intrusion caused me to cough, which only allowed more water to enter my mouth. I struggled, coughing and trying to suck air from my snorkel, but got only more water. I managed to thrash my way to the surface, still hacking and gasping. I looked around desperately to see if I could find the beach, but there was nothing but water. I couldn't even see any other snorkels bobbing around.

Distantly, I could hear the sounds of people shouting and playing music on the beach. Having few other options, I decided to try to swim toward the sound. I was only a middling swimmer even under the best of circumstances, and this was far from ideal. I was still sick, with reduced lung capacity and a hacking cough. That, along with the water I'd breathed, had me working really hard to even stay afloat. I felt like I was only getting the smallest gasps of air, and, with each stroke, more water lapped at my mouth.

As hard as I was trying, it didn't feel like I was getting any closer to the beach sounds. It was the current, I realized; it was pushing me farther and farther out to sea. I was trying to swim but I wasn't stronger than the tide. I paused, panting, and looked around again: still nothing but sunshine and beautiful blue water. Even the Jet Skis had gone off somewhere else. I realized that even if I managed to get the air necessary to shout, no one would be able to hear me. No one was going to come help me. No one could even see that I was drowning just feet away from them.

Wait—I was *drowning?*

Yes, that's what they call it when you're sucking water into your lungs, you can't get any air, and you're flailing around desperately far from shore. The moment I acknowledged this, I felt a rush of panic overwhelm me. It was at least as physical as it was mental—maybe even more physical. As soon as that panic hit me, it was as though I suddenly lost all buoyancy and dropped like a rock, straight down toward the ocean floor. It wasn't even that deep—maybe ten or twelve feet down—but it felt like being buried alive. I touched the beautiful white sand of the ocean floor and looked up at the distant sunlight and all I could feel was that panic completely overwhelming me. It was the panic I was drowning in, just as much as the water.

Then I had a thought, one clearer and even more powerful than the realization that I was drowning: *Scott, this isn't going to happen.*

It was just one thought, but it was clear and forceful, and it rose out of the clamoring panic, so I grabbed it with both hands.

This isn't going to happen. You are not going to drown today.

I used the thought like a weapon to beat back the panic. I braced my feet against the sand and pushed off, heading up toward the sunlight. When I broke the surface, I took a gasping, coughing breath and immediately started pushing myself toward those same beach sounds. I was still fighting the current, and it was hard—even harder than before, if that was possible—but I never allowed myself to think I wouldn't make it. There was a part of me that was tired and in pain and so acutely aware of how far I was from shore, but I pushed those feelings down as firmly as I could. *You are not going to drown,* I told myself; I *demanded* it of myself.

I don't think I've ever felt better in my life than when my foot hit the sandy bottom and I was able to stand up. I staggered out of the ocean and onto an entirely new section of beach. After sitting down for a moment to catch my breath, I realized I was just around a small bend from where my wife and friends were sitting. I had been practically in front of them the whole time.

I approached them at a run, adrenaline still pumping through my body.

"It's okay," I laughed at their confused faces. "I made it!"

I gave my wife a big, certainly sandy, wet hug, much to her befuddlement.

"Made what?" she asked. "Where were you?"

I looked from her to the other people on the beach and saw the same puzzled look. They had no idea anything had happened to me. My whole life-or-death struggle had taken place in maybe ten or fifteen minutes. For them, I had just gone for a quick snorkel and come back strangely chipper. I thought for a moment what it would have looked like from an outside perspective. My near-drowning would have simply appeared to be a slightly awkward dive and a short swim back to shore. I had been truly alone out there. It was a moment when I'd had no one to rely on but myself, and, to my everlasting relief, I had come through.

"It's nothing," I told my wife, flopping down on the sand next to her. "I'll tell you all about it later."

I've heard it said that not only do people change their lives or ways of thinking after an intense personal experience, but that it is also, in fact, the only reliable way that people change their ways of thinking. People change religions, switch political affiliations, quit lifelong habits, or establish new ones after a significant or traumatic experience, and something like that happened to me, though perhaps not as intensely. I didn't suddenly quit my job to become a laid-back beach bro or anything, but my experience in the ocean that day did lead me to reevaluate the way I was living.

It was the first step down the road to learning how to harness my hyperfocus instead of letting it lead me around. I needed to be a better caretaker for my entire life, not just the parts of it that involved a camera. It wasn't just that I'd been momentarily oblivious to danger in the water that morning; it was a whole series of things that contributed to a dangerous situation. I was in suboptimal health in the first place because I wasn't listening to my body. And I was fixated on my camera because I knew of no other way to just comfortably be and enjoy myself. It was a chain of problems, a series of mistakes that compounded, and, in that moment, three wheels weren't enough.

In many ways, I was lucky. I had survived, of course, without any damage, and my crash had been a relatively small one. It *could* have been much worse, but it wasn't. I've seen other people, however, who've had the moment when the instability catches up to them and does much more lasting damage: broken marriages, health problems, even—ironically—professional failure. When the crash occurs, it can take down the whole car, even the parts upon which we've lavished so much attention.

I didn't necessarily know all these things as I sat there in the sand and let the sun dry me off that day, but I did have a sense that I'd learned *something.* At the very least, I'd come away with a sense of just how powerful my ability to focus can be. Yes, I've eventually come to see this incident as a result of negative hyperfocus, but that same ability to home in on one thing and force everything else out was also what saved me that day. Fixating on that single idea—*you will not drown today*—allowed me to push aside the panic and get myself to safety. Hyperfocus did that for me.

I come back to that moment often in my life when I'm facing a big personal or professional challenge. When anxiety or uncertainty threaten to cloud my mind, I think to myself, *If you panic, you drown.* That helps me refocus; it helps me find my one goal and keep moving toward it, even when it's hard. Even when it feels impossible.

I like this story because I think it is ultimately a tale of balance and stability, and what hurts our capacity for those things. The human body floats, but we have to do it consciously; we have to *decide* to float and relax. If we struggle, if we gasp, if we panic, we become hopelessly unbalanced, and we sink. The same principle works in our lives. Things are not going to naturally balance themselves; we have to make a concerted effort to create some kind of equilibrium.

We don't have to do it all on our own either. If I'd had a life preserver—hell, even a pool float—that day in the ocean,

I would have grabbed it immediately. There are tools that help us balance, and we should find the ones that work for us and use them. For me, designated "Free Days" are a tool that helps stabilize me. They ensure that I don't get back into a mind-set where anything that is not directly related to work goes on the back burner. I also use my periodic "Free Days" to pursue interests totally outside of photography to make sure that I am thinking and developing in new ways. Medication, coaching, exercise, delegating responsibilities: these are all tools I use to keep myself afloat.

Another thing I learned in the water that day is that drowning doesn't look or sound like drowning. It's not someone splashing wildly and shouting for help. Drowning occurs inside your head when you let that panic take over, and you can sink without ever making a sound. It's the same way in our work and in our lives. How often have you gotten in over your head? Agreed to a project that was too much for you and buried yourself without acknowledging it? When you finally allow yourself to realize that you've committed to something you can't do, you've probably felt a sensation pretty similar to what I experienced as I was plummeting toward the ocean floor.

Most of us, however, don't express any of this—not the mounting concerns and fears, and certainly not the panic—until it is way too late. Entrepreneurs in particular, those "rugged individualists," never want to show weakness or admit when they are overleveraged in some way. Unfortunately, the practical outcome of this is that you can drown on dry land, and, just like in the water, it can happen so quietly that no one else notices—and no one reaches out to help.

This is another area in which we have to fight that tendency to hyperfocus. We have to consciously pause and check in with ourselves. Is this too much? Am I capable of completing this? Will this timeline work? And, if the answer to these questions is "no," we have to ask ourselves what we are going to do to get to shore. If panic is not an option, the only thing left to do is survive, and that is where we need to direct our focus. Panic, like hyperfocus, is not a purely negative response. In fact, panic is supposed to keep us alive. It can make us move when we need to get away or make us freeze when we need to go unseen. At the very least, it is a profound warning that something has gone wrong and we need to fix it. We can't completely ignore or dismiss our panic, but we can't let it run the show either. We need to balance those intense feelings just as we balance our work and our time.

> Entrepreneurs have to consciously pause and check in: is this too much?

The oldest and most trustworthy tool for stabilizing a camera is a tripod. You've undoubtedly seen them; they're invaluable for slow-speed exposure, nature photography, and reducing motion blur in the final image. Tripods come in all sizes, from elaborate rigs for video cameras to tiny, lightweight travel versions. They've been part of the photographer's tool

> We need to balance those intense feelings just as we balance our work and our time.

kit from the very beginning, but to me, the most interesting thing about them is that they require multiple points of contact with the ground to work. I believe that's a perfect representation of how to balance our professional ambitions and passions with functional needs and the less definable personal work that needs to take place in our lives: we should never rely on just one thing. Just like a tripod is more stable than a bowling pin, dispersing our attention and hard work into multiple parts of our lives makes for a solid surface upon which we can safely rest.

CHAPTER 10

– Contact Sheets –
Getting a Second Opinion

If you've ever had professional photos taken, perhaps for a wedding or high school senior portrait, you probably consulted a contact sheet at some point in that process. A contact sheet is a sheet of paper with thumbnail-sized images of all the photos from a given shoot, and its purpose is to give the client the opportunity to choose his or her favorites.

Traditionally, contact sheets were made by exposing the photo negatives on a sheet of photo paper, but with digital technology, they've become nearly obsolete. Today, you're more likely to get an email with a link to download all your images because it's just so much easier. Even if you shoot on film, you'll scan your negatives to create digital files. Either way, however, the goal is the same: to allow the client some input on the project.

Many photographers like contact sheets for their aesthetic appeal, and because it makes visual comparison between similar shots a little easier, but more than almost any of the other settings or accoutrements we've talked about in this book, contact sheets are for the client. When you hire someone to photograph your fiftieth wedding anniversary or the birth of your child, you are placing a lot of trust in that person. The photos he or she takes—or chooses not to take—will shape memories of that event for years to come. For most people, there will probably come a time when photos are all that remain of that particular moment, so it makes perfect sense that people would want to be involved in some way with that process. By selecting certain images and discarding others, the client is able to make a choice about what they want to highlight and what they can safely forget. They are defining the day on their own terms, and in a certain sense, shaping their reality.

Contact sheets are a more literal, tactile version of something that we all do every day: We make choices about our reality. We decide how we see ourselves and how we want to be seen. We are all constantly curating not only the way we present to the outside world, but also our perception of ourselves and who we are as people. This has only become more true with the rise of social media and the development of digital identities. Before the culture of living online really took off, we might have encountered contact sheets maybe once or twice a decade. Maybe we'd use them for an engagement, headshots for a job, a holiday celebration, or some other big occasion that needed to be recorded for posterity.

> Contact sheets are a literal version of something that we do every day: make choices about our reality.

Today, however, I am sure that your Facebook News Feed is filled with photos of restaurant dishes and other evidence of your friends' everyday lives. Nowadays every moment is special enough to be photographed extensively. We then select our favorite versions of ourselves, and after a judicious application of filters, post them on the internet, where everyone can see our lives the way we want them to be seen.

I don't mean this as a criticism (well, not *just* as a criticism). I think much of what we do online is just a heightened version of the editing and shaping that people do in their heads all the time. We don't have a pure, objectively correct understanding of ourselves or our lives; in fact, in many ways it's literally *impossible* for us to have that because of how our bodies and brains work. Have you ever listened to a recording of your own voice and been surprised by how unfamiliar it sounds? That's because we cannot hear ourselves speak the way other people do.

The human ear hears sounds in two basic ways: bone conduction and air conduction. Air conduction, the way we hear most sounds and other people's voices, occurs when sound waves in the air vibrate the eardrum, which passes that information along to the inner ear. Bone conduction takes place when a vibration goes directly through the skull to the inner ear without touching the eardrum. Because these two processes are subtly different, they produce distinct sounds—generally making our own voices sound lower pitched to us than they do to others.

It's sort of eerie and a little sad to think about that. It also raises a question: What is our "real" voice, anyway? Is it the voice we hear when we speak, or the voice others hear? Who gets to decide who we are? Are we defined by our personal sense of ourselves, or how other people see us? Is the person on our Instagram feed more or less real than the one who looks back at us from the bathroom mirror? Who should be in charge of picking the best, most representative images from our personal contact sheet?

This chapter is probably the most personal in this book, and I wanted to share it with you because I think too many people—not just entrepreneurs—aren't using their own contact sheets properly. Often, we aren't very deliberate or even conscious about the choices we make for ourselves. Instead, we fall into roles rather than selecting them, and we rarely stop to think about how we envision ourselves: who we are trying to be, who we should be or can't be or even believe ourselves to be. Often we let other people do all the selecting, or we go too far in the opposite direction and refuse any outside input. As I said before, I don't think anybody has a perfectly accurate perception of him- or herself, but we can have a more—or less—healthy one.

In my case, I had a perception of myself that hadn't changed much since early childhood. I was "the camera guy," and that was all I needed. As long as I could keep photography centralized in my life, it didn't matter so much that I struggled with other things or seemed to process things differently from the people around me. For me, it took outsider input to begin to change that self-perception. I needed an expert to look at my life and characteristics—all the "snapshots" of me—and find a pattern that had been hidden there all along.

When you look through the contact sheet for an event, what you are really doing is selecting a narrative for that day. I needed a narrative for my life—or rather, I needed a different narrative than the one I had, which was basically just that I was fundamentally incapable of certain things and I couldn't ever expect to change. That narrative couldn't come from me or from the people closest to me because we'd all accepted the idea that my limitations were fixed and permanent—just part of who I am, or even part of how creative people in general are. I hesitate to say it was a "false" narrative because it was my reality for a long time, but it certainly wasn't the *only* narrative that was possible. In some ways, our lives are like a Rorschach test: different people can look at the same inkblot on paper and see completely different things.

For example, imagine a recently married woman is perusing the contact sheet from her wedding to pick the ones she'll have printed. She chooses to include the one where the groom dances with his mother and not the one where he does a keg stand at the reception. She picks the shot of the best man fixing her new husband's tie and not the one of him high-fiving all the groomsmen. She wants all the photos of her and her husband posed immaculately under the gazebo and none of the garter toss. This new bride is choosing a narrative about her wedding, and also about her husband. She presents him as a dignified, elegant man marrying the love of his life in a fairytale ceremony. Is it true? Well, the photos are all right there; they are records of things that happened. If she'd made the opposite choice at every turn, she'd be telling a visual story about a carefree, maybe somewhat immature guy having fun on his wedding day, and that would be just as true. The pictures—the bits of basic information—remain the same; it's all about the structure and the narrative into which you slot them.

Here's another story: After Dan Sullivan first suggested that I might have ADHD, it took me a year to actually make and keep an appointment with a psychiatrist. *A year.* I put it off and then forgot about it for a long stretch of time. I cancelled several appointments, and I missed a couple more. When I finally made it to the appointment, I was fifteen minutes late because I'd gotten lost on the way to the doctor's office.

I didn't consider any of this to be weird or bad behavior. It was just how I was—scrambled, flaky, absentminded, or whatever you want to call it. It was the way I had been since childhood. I knew other people didn't seem to have such a hard time with things like prioritizing tasks and keeping appointments . . . but other people were also good at memorizing dates in history class or formulas in math class. Different strokes, right?

I apologized, of course, for being late and all my previous cancellations.

"You canceled?" the psychiatrist said, not accusingly, but interested.

"Yeah, three times."

He raised an eyebrow at that, but I didn't yet know enough about ADHD to realize I was describing a pretty common behavior for people with the disorder.

"And I noticed you were a few minutes late," he said. "Did you have trouble finding the place?"

I laughed.

"Oh, yeah. I couldn't find the sign and I had to circle the parking lot a few times, but I found it eventually. I always do."

It was true; sometimes I had to leave twenty minutes early, or make my peace with arriving ten minutes late, but I always got where I was going. The people who were close to me knew to build in extra time or to offer themselves as navigators for just that reason.

From there we segued into a conversation about driving, and he asked me if I'd ever been in any accidents. I'd been in three, all front-end collisions and all my fault. I hadn't been texting or impaired or anything; I'd just zoned out and missed something in a critical moment.

"I'm a lot better now that I've got my shiny, new BMW though," I assured him. "I'm super cautious with that."

"Oh? You got a new car?"

"Yeah, it was a last-minute kinda thing. Just went out and got a BMW."

"Really?

"Yeah, I just came home with it one day. My wife was pretty surprised, I can tell you."

While we were talking, my knee was bouncing up and down relentlessly. It happened all the time, so much that I barely even registered the motion. But then the psychiatrist pointed at my leg.

"Scott, are you aware you're jiggling your leg like that?"

I looked down and, just for a second, it almost felt like my leg belonged to someone else. I *hadn't* been aware, actually.

In retrospect, it's almost funny how perfectly I was embodying ADHD tendencies: distractibility, challenges with time management, memory issues, fidgeting, impulsivity. I could have been on a poster for Adderall! As far as I was concerned, though, we were just having a normal conversation, and I was kind of wondering when he was going to conduct the ADHD test.

None of this information was a secret. People in my life had observed all these things about me, and I certainly knew I had these habits and this history. It was people like that psychiatrist and Dan Sullivan who were able, because of their education and backgrounds, to look at the exact same set of "pictures" of me and find a different story. Parents, teachers, friends, and relatives had all looked at my contact sheet and picked out the "eccentric artist" story. For the first time, however, someone was able to offer me a narrative with a different ending. The "untreated ADHD" story was more open-ended than the eccentric-artist story, and more hopeful. The story my psychiatrist offered had room for change, for growth and improvement, and it also offered me a certain amount of grace.

Being able to understand my instincts and actions within the framework of ADHD made it a lot easier to find and accept help for those areas in which I struggled. Instead of thinking of myself as just fundamentally unable to do certain things, I learned how to look for other ways to accomplish the same goals. As many experts in treating ADHD say, it's not about trying harder; it's about trying *differently*. There is a lot of power in that way of thinking, and it changed how I thought about mistakes and failure. If I was struggling to do something, it didn't necessarily mean I couldn't do it—only that I'd not yet found the "Scott way" to get it done. Sometimes it *did* mean that I wasn't the best person to do it—but that was a form of grace as well. Being able to acknowledge that I was genuinely suited to some things more than others—and that it was okay to ask for help when I needed it—was a revelation.

Being able to pull back from a challenge and know that it's not about doing everything the way someone else would do it, but about getting it done, period, has been vital in terms of managing my business. It took me a long time to realize, for example, that I am not good at taking customer service calls. It is not something I enjoy, and especially before I started treating my ADHD, following intricate conversations and maintaining lots of details in my head without actually doing anything was basically my kryptonite. It took me years to realize that if I was bad at that part of running a business and it made me miserable, it was okay to hand it off to someone else. Recognizing ADHD's role in my life and being able to accept other accommodations allowed me to let go of that small thing. And it really was a small thing, but delegating it to someone else made everyone's lives better.

Entrepreneurs and people with ADHD (and of course, the big group in the middle of that Venn diagram) often have high expectations for themselves. We think big and we think a lot, but the flip side of having a constant stream of big ideas is that it can be extremely difficult to understand and accept that we can't act on all of them all the time. Finding a way to focus on one thing at a time, and to be okay with "slowing down" in that way, is vital for avoiding burnout and self-destruction. Learning to accept our differences and work with them rather than fighting them is a lifelong process, and it's even harder with ADHD or any other "invisible disability."

> Finding a way to focus on one thing at a time is vital for avoiding burnout and self-destruction.

Executive-function disorders make it difficult to do the things that "should" be easy—listening to someone talk, remembering to get milk at the grocery store, finishing simple tasks—and that causes people to beat themselves up for having trouble with those things. Often, outsiders see these struggles as unimportant or the result of bad choices. That mentality makes it very easy for people to pass judgment on the adaptations and strategies we use to cope with these problems. If a person who uses a wheelchair takes an elevator rather than the stairs to get to the second floor of a building, no one says that is in any way illegitimate or unnecessary. Everyone recognizes that that's someone using alternate means to accomplish a goal. Yet, if someone with autism or a sensory-processing disorder wears headphones at work, or if someone with ADHD requires important communication to be put in writing, many people look sideways at them. These things aren't seen as needs like the elevator is, but as ways of somehow getting one up on everyone else—as though if people just tried hard enough, they wouldn't need any special considerations.

Which brings me to medication, particularly Adderall, which is possibly the most controversial ADHD medication—

and the one I take. Ten or fifteen years ago, Ritalin had its time in the barrel; many people were concerned that it was over-prescribed to children and was turning them into zombies. Ritalin is still in wide use, but Adderall has supplanted it as the drug that inspires the most handwringing, mainly because it has become more and more commonly abused, particularly in the context of work or school. Adderall has become a running joke, shorthand for something you take to boost yourself through finals week, much in the same way that "being ADHD" is a colloquial way to say you're distracted. But the widespread abuse of Adderall (just like the misapplication of the term ADHD) only makes it harder for people who actually need treatment to get it without stigma.

These days, when you tell someone you take Adderall for ADHD, you're likely to get a few basic types of response:

- "Oh yeah, I love Adderall. One time in college, I stayed up for four days on that stuff!"
- "So you're a drug-addict, then? And you made up a disease to get scripts?"
- "Ugh, don't you know how bad Adderall is for you? Have you tried managing your ADHD with diet and exercise?"

People don't always put it so crudely, but lots of people treat ADHD medication in general, and Adderall in partic-ular, with an extreme degree of skepticism that isn't applied to other treatments. No one ever tells diabetics they're going to get addicted to insulin if they keep taking it every day. People don't automatically doubt that you have a cold when they see you taking cough syrup, just because some other people abuse it. People don't opine about whether or not you've been brainwashed into merely *thinking* you have heart disease when you take a blood-pressure pill. But all of these things happen when people learn you are on medication for ADHD.

I am not going to tell you that Adderall, Ritalin, and other stimulant-based medications aren't serious and don't have potential for abuse; they definitely do. However, the widespread willingness to shame people for using these medications is out of proportion to their risks. The difference between a medication and a drug is in the use of it, and many important lifesaving medications can also be abused. Benzodiazepines can ease anxiety disorders, but they can also produce a heroin-like high. Powerful mood stabilizers like lithium can be lifesavers for people with bipolar disorder or other mood disorders, but they can also be habit-forming when abused. And, of course, we've all seen in the last couple of decades how deadly opioid pain relievers can be when used inappropriately.

Unlike many of those other drugs, however, Adderall has been defined by the worst uses people put it to. It has this reputation as basically being prescription cocaine, but when used correctly, it's nothing like that. To return to our example of the person using a wheelchair, imagine a fully able-bodied person who regularly rides around in a wheelchair because, he says, "If I use my arms and legs to propel myself, I can go really fast! This is so fun!" That is roughly what it's like when a person without ADHD abuses Adderall. Sure, maybe it gives you some sort of boost, but I take it simply to get to "normal."

That's a critical piece of the puzzle that is often missing from the general conversation about ADHD: that it is actually a physiological difference in the structure of the brain. I said before that ADHD is an "invisible disability," but it's actually perfectly visible if you have an MRI. ADHD brains are structurally distinct from "normal" ones, and respond differently to stimuli. People with ADHD have different levels of important brain chemicals and respond differently to them when they are produced, and that means medications work differently on them. Just as a person with perfectly functioning kidneys doesn't need to take insulin (and if they did, it would probably hurt them), someone without those physical differences does not need Adderall, and it acts on them not as a treatment, but as an intoxicant.

I wanted to talk about this—about getting diagnosed, and specifically about taking medication—because in my experience, the way we talk about ADHD in our society is bad for people with the disorder. The stereotypes and stigma surrounding both ADHD as a concept *and* specific meds taken to manage it often keep people from getting diagnosed, from being open about it once they do know they have ADHD, and even from getting the treatment that might be most effective for them.

I am not saying that everyone has to take Adderall; there is a range of medications, including non-stimulant types, that help people with ADHD. There are also a lot of strides being made in terms of specialized behavioral therapy and coaching focused on executive-function disorders. Even those who ask that annoying question, "Have you tried yoga?" have something of a point: exercise and other lifestyle choices can also help manage symptoms. People should do what works for them, but I hate to see people struggling unnecessarily because they are afraid of being seen as a "drug seeker," or are afraid the meds will change who they are as a person. For most people, no one solution can do it all. It's almost always a combination of treatments that work together to help you clear hurdles you might once have believed were unchangeable parts of your personal landscape.

For years, people told me that I should take meditation. A lot of smart people whom I admire advocate meditating every day; they say it works wonders in terms of settling them down and helping them focus. For years, I tried really hard to meditate. I got apps, I took a class, and I bought a book about it (which I intended to read but never actually did), but nothing helped. No matter how hard I tried, I could never get past the "clear your mind" step. My mind was extremely cluttered, and more ideas were pouring in every second.

I began to honestly believe that I couldn't meditate, that I was incapable of it, and the thought was extremely frustrating. You mean I can't sit in a room and not do anything? It's literally the easiest task imaginable! Whenever I tried to meditate with other people, I'd get weird looks: Why couldn't I stay still? Why couldn't I focus? What was wrong with me? Eventually I quit trying meditation just as I quit trying the other seemingly "easy" things that I found inexplicably impossible.

Years later, after diagnosis and treatment, I was in my pool at my vacation home in New Hampshire on a peaceful summer day. The sun was setting and no one else was around; it was pure peace and quiet. It was about five o'clock, which would have been Jack Daniels o'clock in the old days, but now I was able to just float there and relax without the help of a drink or two. I slipped into meditation almost accidentally; it was the first time in my life that I really understood what people mean when they say, "Let your mind go blank." I'd never had that experience before; it isn't physically possible without Adderall.

I started meditating regularly, and I found that it actually did do a lot of the cool things all those smart people said it did. It helped me center myself and focus and maintain calm. It became another tool I could use to manage my ADHD, but it only works in conjunction with medication—just as a zoom lens is a great tool, but it's only useful if it actually fits on your camera. The suggestions that people offered me were one piece of a puzzle—one snapshot in a contact sheet—and by picking through them and making conscious choices about how I see myself, I was able to put together the image of a more successful, happier person.

Knowing who we are isn't just a process of discovery; it's a construction project. We build ourselves from the pieces of information available to us, just like a bride plucking fairytale moments from a contact sheet. The most important thing is that you understand who is holding the contact sheet, who is making those choices and building that persona for you. Allowing others some input is vital, but we also have to be able to pause and check in on ourselves as well.

There's a funny quirk that most photographers I've met all seem to possess: we don't love having our pictures taken. I can't count the number of times someone has told me something like, "Oh, I'm always behind the camera, so I never get photographed." Often, that's a choice, whether or not people are conscious of it. Part of what drew me to photographing family functions was a desire to remove myself from the picture, to get outside of the interpersonal interactions that I found stressful. I'm not unique in this regard; behind the camera can be a great hiding place. The problem with a really good hiding place, though, is that sometimes

> We build ourselves from the pieces of information available, just like plucking moments from a contact sheet.

you start to hide even from yourself. It's important, every once in a while, to snap a few selfies and remind yourself who you really are.

CHAPTER 11

– Bracketing –
What's Your Plan B?

Sometimes, no matter how carefully you manage your settings and plan for a shot, there's just no substitute for actually taking the picture to see how it turns out. If you're not sure exactly which combination of exposure settings will give you the clearest image, or if there are multiple parts of a scene you'd like to highlight, it makes sense to bracket your shots.

Bracketing is the practice of taking multiple versions of the same photo, adjusting the settings each time to create a different effect in the final image. It's similar to the concept of "coverage" in video production: filming a scene from multiple angles to make sure that there's a wide array of shots an editor can use when cutting together the final product. Bracketing developed as a common practice because photographers recognized two fundamental truths about their work (and work in general):

1. The moment is fleeting. The light is always shifting, living things are always moving, the atmosphere is never static, and the image you want to capture may only exist for a few precious seconds. You want to get as much usable material as you can—*while* you still can—because the scene may not be available for a "do-over."

2. Something can always go wrong. You may be absolutely certain that a shot requires a certain aperture or ISO, but your eye can be fooled, your experience can lead you astray, and the visuals can be more complicated than you realize. If you're shooting on film, you may not even realize you've chosen incorrectly until you develop the photos and see that they are over- or underexposed.

Bracketing is to photography as "Measure twice; cut once" is to woodworking. Most photographers bracket their shots reflexively, and many modern cameras even have built-in bracketing systems that automate the whole process.

If only we could all be so rigorous about having a plan B in other areas of life. Because that's all bracketing really is: the acknowledgment that something may not turn out as planned, and a secondary strategy to allow for that.

Early in my career I worked as a photographer for a newspaper in Boston, and the importance of bracketing was drilled into my head there. The news doesn't stop or loop back around for second chances; if I missed a shot, I had failed. I diligently bracketed every scene I photographed because if I didn't get the shot that the paper needed, I didn't get paid.

When I moved on to other types of photography, those early lessons stayed with me. Even in my most hardcore, rugged-individualist, go-it-alone days, my photography training made me wary of taking on any challenge without preparing a backup plan. In some ways, my insistence on doing everything myself actually encouraged me to make more contingency plans. I was acutely aware of the fact that it was just me out there, and if I came up short, either in my equipment or in my abilities, there was no one to pick up the slack.

> Acknowledge that something may not turn out as planned, and have a plan B to allow for that.

A lifetime of compensating for my ADHD (even if I didn't realize that was exactly what I was doing) also made me a little more likely than the average person to have a backup plan. I was used to doing things like buying copies of important items because I might misplace them, or giving myself extra time to travel somewhere in case I got lost on the way. I did these things without really thinking about them, much in the way an integrated digital camera will bracket your shots automatically. It may seem counterintuitive; I had a disorder that made it harder for me to be organized, which in turn forced me to be *more* organized in certain ways than some "normal" folks. I didn't have the luxury of assuming I'd remember everything or wouldn't make mistakes, and the steps I took to protect myself against those potential problems had the added benefit of mitigating the damage from other issues that were outside of my control.

This personal practice of "bracketing" my professional life has saved my bacon more times than I could tell you about, even if this were a much longer book. But perhaps the most memorable occasion on which I rescued my business using a plan B occurred a few years ago. I had been doing some green-screen work and promotional photography for a number of HBO shows, and on this particular day, I was working on a promotional shoot for *Game of Thrones*. The idea was to create a unique experience for the sponsors and HBO executives who were attending this event: We would take green-screen photos of them and composite those images into stills from the show itself, giving each participant a takeaway photo to have as a keepsake. Essentially, we were inserting them into their favorite show!

I was particularly scattered that day because I had a lot of different subprojects to track. The overarching contract was with HBO, but each show and each advertising campaign required its own shoot, which necessitated its own plan, equipment, and materials. To get a handle on what I knew would be a complicated and stressful job with lots of moving parts, my main strategy was to always have two of any mission-critical components: If I was storing photos, I had two forms of storage. If I was editing, I had two computers. If I was shooting, I had two cameras. Everything had a backup, just in case.

On the day of the *Game of Thrones* shoot, I very nearly left my office without one of those backups: my second laptop, which was intended to serve as an alternate for my primary computer. I'm not sure what stopped me in the doorway—maybe some instinct from a lifetime of forgotten items, or just the habit I'd developed over the years of loading myself down with everything I could possibly need before I left for a job—but I *did* stop, and turned around to grab my other laptop.

This particular shoot was very important for a number of reasons: *Game of Thrones* was definitely HBO's flagship series at the time, and one that required a lot of green-screen work because of the nature of the show. We also had a lot of high-profile people on set, and I don't just mean the actors. The point people for the advertising department—the people who would determine whether or not I got any future contracts with HBO—were there as well. The technical complexity and scope of the project would have made it a little nerve-racking even without potentially lucrative future clients watching my performance the whole time.

We had all the physical components set up, and I opened my computer to launch the program that I used to create and edit the green-screen photos . . . only to see an ominous pop-up. It said something about an "FBI WARNING!!!"

I felt like my stomach had dropped down to my knees; I knew instantly that it was some sort of virus. I tried to click away from the pop-up, but the mouse was disabled. I had a reasonably good knowledge of computers—professionally, it was a skill I'd had to develop—but I didn't know how to resolve this problem. I certainly couldn't fix it in the next two minutes, which was the amount of time we had before everyone assembled started asking what was taking so long.

I gathered my team, some of whom immediately panicked. One person was even convinced that the FBI was actually investigating us and had disabled my computer for some reason. I looked over at another team member, named Marie, and we instantly reached an understanding. I had shared with her my philosophy that "If you panic, you drown," and I could see from the look on her face that she was keeping herself calm, and trusting that I had some sort of fix for this problem.

As it turned out, I did: the second laptop I had so fortuitously remembered at the last minute. I dug it out of my bag, started it up, and successfully launched our program. "What about the graphics?" Marie whispered to me, referring to the image backgrounds and elements we had designed and gotten approved by HBO weeks before. Without those files, we would not be able to create composites with the pictures I was going to take that day, and we wouldn't be able to deliver what the client was expecting.

When discussing things like sports training or learning to play a musical instrument, people often talk about "muscle memory." The term is a bit of a misnomer—no matter how much we work out, our muscles don't have brains and can't remember things—but if you do the same action in the same way enough times, your brain will create a long-term memory of that action. Eventually, when triggered by the correct stimuli, your brain will make you perform that action without conscious thought. You can clearly see why this would desirable, for example, in combat sports: Who is more likely to win a fight, the person who sees their opponent throw a punch and takes a moment to decide to raise their hand to guard their face . . . or the person who has trained their brain and body to do this automatically? When fractions of seconds matter, muscle memory can mean the difference between a win and a knockout.

I mention this because I think it is applicable to more than just punching people. My lifetime of bracketing not only my shots, but also everything concerning my work created a kind of muscle memory; I would make alternate plans without really thinking about it. In this case, it turned out that I had stored a backup of all our graphics files on a USB flash drive, which I had in my pocket. I barely remembered doing that, but as soon as we had those files approved, some part of my brain must have said, "Back that up right now!" We still had to act quickly and do a little rebuilding in order to load all the saved files onto my laptop, but the shoot proceeded more or less on schedule.

In addition to the advertising people, there were also some HBO execs on the set. We tried to give off an unhurried, confident vibe, acting as though everything were going exactly to plan (which, it was . . . just not the A plan). To this day, I don't think anyone on that set outside my team knew what was going on or how close we came to wasting lots of money and time—which, for tightly scheduled people like actors and television execs, are basically the same thing. If we had let on that there was a problem, even if we'd been able to solve it, the added pressure and frustration from others on the set could only have held things up. I kept the details of the problem and how we were fixing it strictly "need to know," and that allowed us to work faster and more productively.

Camera manufacturers started building automated bracketing features into their products because they knew that consumers wanted that "muscle-memory effect." We want to have buffers, backups, and plan Bs in place without having to think about it. I recently had an enlightening conversation with another photographer. She was in her early thirties and hadn't heard the term *bracketing* (though, to be fair, she was confused at first by my Boston accent, which turns the word into something that sounds more like "brag-a-ding"). When I explained what it was, she, of course, understood the concept of taking a photo in different modes and even pointed out that the iPhone's "Live Photos" feature essentially serves that purpose for even the most casual photos. Bracketing is pervasive in photography, but it has become so ingrained that it doesn't even really register anymore as a physical action or a thought process.

Interestingly enough, catering to this need has created the same problem that we often see with any helpful technology: overreliance. Some younger photographers who have always had the option of using auto-bracketing cameras are neglecting the practice of bracketing manually, even for fleeting or complex shots. This can lead to obvious problems if the bracketing feature doesn't work quite right or doesn't select the exposure settings that the photographer really wanted or needed. More important—to me, at least—is the loss of that instinct to plan ahead and develop contingencies. Being able to strategize and have a plan B at the ready is a crucial skill, and no one has yet developed an auto-bracketing feature for real life.

This, for those of us old enough to remember the earliest word processors, reminds me of the autosave problem. A whole generation of people learned to manually save their documents at regular intervals like it was a religious ritual. We all felt the pain of losing a chunk of homework or a big paper because Word crashed and we hadn't clicked the little floppy-disk icon recently enough. Much like floppy discs themselves, however, manual save was soon rendered moot by technological advancements. Today, almost any word-processing program will autosave your progress, and some even create backups when you make changes. People rarely manually save now because the autosave function works perfectly—except when it doesn't, which is why most people in data security or even just in tech will advise you to back up everything that is important to you, preferably in multiple locations and formats.

> A crucial skill is to strategize and have a plan B at the ready, and no one has developed auto-bracketing for real life.

Features like autosave and auto-exposure bracketing can lull us into a false sense of security: If the machine does the work for us, why bother building up the muscle memory ourselves? The problem isn't about technology; it's about relying too much in general on one thing. I see a very similar issue in highly competent, highly driven people who presume that because they are generally successful, they don't really need a backup plan. Confidence, like most things, is great in moderation and poisonous in excess.

I was able to save that HBO shoot because I never relied exclusively on one thing. I developed a strategy to ensure that no piece of equipment or individual person (including me) was completely indispensable. All these preparations and modes of thinking came very naturally to me when I was working on a shoot; the challenge for me was to learn to bracket my career in general.

I had been going from assignment to assignment, rarely pausing to formulate a bigger picture, let alone to figure out how I might build a safety net around that big picture. Because I wasn't providing any backups or contingencies, I was tacitly relying on myself to resolve any and all problems that might arise in the course of building my business. I was relying more on myself than I would ever rely on a hard drive, but for a long time, it felt totally normal. After all, isn't that what it means to be an entrepreneur: to do everything yourself?

For me, learning to truly bracket my professional future was an outgrowth of learning to visualize my future in detail. Instead of a nebulous desire for "growth," I had to actually decide where I wanted my company to be in three, five, or even twenty-five years. Once I was able to picture that goal and set shorter-term objectives that would get me there, it was a simple mental leap to start thinking about potential pitfalls as well. When I'm trying to get a certain shot, I start just the same way: I visualize my desired end product and work backward.

But this process starts long before I bring out my camera. For example, let's say I want to get a shot of a local lighthouse with a certain glow on it. First, I need to consider what must be in place for that to happen: What time of day will provide that light? Which camera settings will be optimal? Where should I position the camera and myself for the best angle? In answering these questions, I build my strategy.

If I know I need the early-morning light to get the orange glow I want, I then check the sunrise times for the coming week and figure out exactly when I must be on the scene. As I nail down each detail, other details fall into place, and I begin the second layer of strategizing: looking for obvious ways my plan could go awry.

Say I've decided that I want to get that sunrise glow and I know that sunrise will be at 5:04 a.m. tomorrow. I could plan to leave my house at 3:30 a.m. to get there on time. The obvious danger here is the small window of time in which the specific light conditions I want will be available. There are a few different contingency plans I could use to reduce that risk: I could decide to leave earlier, or I could pick out some other days on which to shoot if I have to try again. I could even decide to turn the project into a trip and stay overnight closer to the lighthouse in order to make traffic less of a concern. Any one of these solutions would be a fine backup plan, and by putting any of them in place, I am bracketing *before* I bracket.

Most people have the ability to bracket, and they do it in small ways nearly every day. If you keep an extra shirt in your office or buy three different kinds of yogurt because you forgot which brand your partner likes, you are bracketing. The problem is one of scale. We have no problem acknowledging that something might go wrong when we're talking about not having a change of clothes or buying groceries, but it can be scary to admit to ourselves that we might encounter problems when trying to achieve our professional dreams.

The situation I found myself in on the *Game of Thrones* shoot is a frightening one; no one wants to be caught in a moment like that. But I never panicked because I knew that I had an alternate plan, and that there was an action I could take to make things better. Bracketing means acknowledging that our business—our work—is not only valuable, but also vulnerable, and it is infinitely better to arm yourself against a possible catastrophe than to pretend that it could never happen to you.

> Our work is valuable and vulnerable... better to arm yourself against a possible catastrophe than pretend it could never happen.

CHAPTER 12

– Color Palette –
Managing Your Mind-set and Mood

Have you ever watched the sun rise? I'm not talking about catching a quick glimpse as you head to work or pausing to look out the kitchen window over breakfast, I mean really, truly sitting down to watch the sky transition from night into day. If you've never had the chance to do it, I recommend finding the time some morning. It only takes a few minutes and it offers one of the finest object lessons you can get in the power of light and color.

When the sun comes up over the horizon and turns the world a succession of pink and orange hues, it isn't just exposing the landscape; it's transforming it. We can viscerally feel the difference between the nighttime world and the daytime one. There's a new energy and a clarity, and our bodies respond to it involuntarily; we want to get up and get out and be a part of this new world. It's enough to make us understand why so many ancient cultures worshipped the sun.

Like those ancient cultures, photographers understand the power of the sun and the opportunities it provides as it moves across the sky. Except, in our case, it's more about specific light conditions and not so much about bountiful crops. A lot can be done with electric lights, and some very cool effects can be produced entirely indoors, but sunshine is still the most powerful and versatile light source available to us. Some light conditions outside are only available for hours, or even minutes, and they aren't really replicable under other circumstances; we still haven't been able to create a sunrise in a lab. Because of this, photographers spend a lot of time chasing the sun and trying to seize those fleeting moments.

You may have heard of the "golden hour," a time just before sunset when the air has a hazy, mellow, golden quality. But there's also the "blue hour," a period after the sun has dipped below the horizon but before the light vanishes completely, when the world is moody and dark but you can still capture sharp, arresting silhouettes. There are dozens of these colorscapes in any given day and a good photographer learns them all.

Light and color are like conjoined twins—similar yet distinct entities that can never be separated from each other. A large part of developing your "eye" as a photographer is learning to work with those two concepts. It's called "blue hour," after all, not "low-light hour." What we want when we go out to capture these distinct moments is not only the unique exposure, but also the colors that are rendered visible by that exposure. We want sunrise pink and sunset red, and we want them because, more than any other single aspect of a photo, color sets the mood of an image.

Human beings are extremely responsive to color and, especially in the Western world, a lot of those responses are fairly predictable and uniform. Here's a pop quiz: without thinking too much about it, name an energetic color. If you are like most Americans, you probably thought of red, or possibly orange, or even yellow. That's because, in Western cultures, we think of those colors as vigorous, energetic, passionate, and "hot." Studies have even shown that people will report feeling physically warmer in a room painted red than in one painted blue or even white.

Different groups of people have different associations with familiar colors, however. For example, most Westerners traditionally see red as inappropriate for a wedding dress and prefer white, to symbolize purity, while in East Asia, red is associated with good luck and ceremony, and white is worn at funerals. Thus, traditional Chinese wedding dresses are typically red, and wearing white was—up until the last few decades—a strange and inappropriate choice.

Even in the United States, we've flipped our perceptions of pink and baby blue just in the last hundred years or so.

Once thought of as a "stronger," more masculine color (and a derivative of red), pink was initially marketed as a color for baby boys. It wasn't until the 1940s that the palette was reversed and clothing manufacturers started designing pink clothing for girls and blue for boys. To many of us, it probably seems natural that pink is a "feminine" color and blue a "masculine" one, but that perception is based almost entirely on eighty years of aggressive advertising and not on any intrinsic quality of the colors themselves. That's why we see such a wide range of feelings about different colors. Orange is a sacred color in Japan, but fun or even silly in the U.S. In Mexico and Poland, purple is the color of envy, while in the U.S. it is green. We all have our own traditions and mores that inform our perceptions.

Some basics of color psychology appear to apply to a wide swath of humanity, however, and I don't think it's any accident that it's mainly the less abstract meanings that are more universal. Not every culture sees blue as masculine, but a great many do see it as "colder" than other colors. Red, the color of fire and blood, is associated with warmth and vitality in many parts of the world, while blue, like the ocean and sky, signifies coldness, wetness, and calm.

A good photographer understands these almost involuntary reactions to color and is able to use color as a tool to evoke certain responses in the viewer. If I want to highlight a subject, I might put the subject in a vibrant color against a subdued background. If I want a photograph to feel kinetic and active, I might incorporate bright, contrasting colors. If I want something nostalgic, I might go for softer, fuzzier hues. I know that lots of green evokes feelings of growth and lushness, while purple suggests opulence and even decadence. Blue measurably lowers people's stress levels, while reds and yellows have been shown to improve athletic performance in some people. I can manipulate the shades and hues as well as the context of the colors to communicate anything I want in the final image.

Understanding the connection between color and emotion is helpful in more than just the artistic sense, however. There is a baseline principle here that can be applied to almost anything in life, and it's not just about the literal colors that surround us. For me, "managing your color palette" in terms of business, your personal life, or any other endeavor really means curating your environment to generate a certain mood or feeling. That might mean repainting the walls or buying new furniture, but it can also mean changing the sonic environment of your workspace or changing the language you use to discuss a project. It's about tweaking those details that maybe we don't even consciously notice to generate a psychological change that makes us more effective and more successful.

Right now, my primary office features deep, vibrant red furniture, the kind that draws the eye the moment you walk in the door. Why? Well, there are actually a few reasons. At the most immediate level, that particular shade of red is what

> "Managing your color palette" means curating your environment to generate a certain mood or feeling.

we might call "Christmas red" or even "Santa red," and that feels appropriate for the business since we are focused so much on the Santa Experience track. For that same reason, I try to wear a little bit of red throughout the month of December (usually a red shirt or sweater and my omnipresent red hiking boots). If we are selling ourselves as purveyors of holiday magic, we should look the part, right? And, in the U.S., that means Santa red.

At a deeper level, red is also a good color for generating creative energy. It is active, warm, and intense; it immediately engages the eye and the mind follows. The fact that I've selected just red furniture and kept it all a consistent shade, however, gives people a visual break. The walls aren't red and the carpet isn't either; it's a pop of color in an otherwise visually restful room. This encourages creativity and excitement without overwhelming people with intense stimuli (something that is very important for me personally).

When I designed my office, I took a lot of inspiration from the offices of people I admire. I found that, in most cases, the people whom I like and look up to have working spaces that are invigorating but not "busy." The artwork was carefully selected and placed with an eye toward visual balance. Whenever you entered one of those spaces, there is a flow to it—a natural progression from one room to another—that makes you settle in almost immediately. I wanted to create that feeling in my office because I wanted to make people comfortable immediately so they could feel free to spitball and collaborate without fear or discomfort.

Naturally, I also like to include photography in my work and personal spaces, and I want to be thoughtful about which pictures I include. My goal is never to find something that simply "looks nice," but to generate feelings, both in the people who visit my office and in myself. I want to inspire myself and encourage focus—get myself into a professional headspace—and because that's something of a moving target, my approach to wall art has changed over the years.

Early on, when I was decorating my personal office at home, I chose a lot of photos (both mine and other photographers') that had an expansive, grandiose feeling. I wanted sweeping landscapes, incredible vistas; I was all about the big, bold statements that made me feel like taking a risk. Building a business from the ground up is a perilous endeavor with a high likelihood of failure, so, at that time in my life, I needed my environment to encourage me to take a leap.

Later, as the business grew and I had more and more success, I started making it a point to put up my favorite or most memorable shots from big projects I'd done. With these photos, I wasn't necessarily trying to choose a particular visual theme so much as I was selecting the image that would immediately remind me of a specific assignment. What I ended up with was kind of a time machine effect such that walking down the hall at my office sent me back months or years as I briefly relived each experience. This provides a sense of history and continuity and gives me a valuable context for the work I do.

Creating an atmosphere conducive to the kind of work you want to do is about more than just visual elements, however. We are constantly getting all sorts of input from all five senses, and that input goes a long way in helping us develop an idea of what a given space is supposed to be "for." For example, if you entered a room where club music was blaring from trembling speakers, you would probably conclude that you weren't in the boardroom. Similarly, if you walked into a bathroom and smelled cookies baking, you'd probably be pretty confused. Even very simple things like adjusting the temperature of a room or eliminating echo can have a huge impact upon how people feel—and thus how they perform—in that space.

Beyond the physical elements of a workplace, it's also important to be thoughtful about our own actions and especially our language. The way we speak about something has an enormous power to shape that thing, and even relatively minor tweaks to our vocabulary can completely reframe a conversation or concept. That's the reason I prefer "team member" to "employee." It may seem like a small distinction, but it can actually put people in a very different headspace. The more I use that language, the more it becomes a part of my thought pattern.

A few years ago, I had the chance to talk with John Jacobs, CEO of Life Is Good, and he impressed upon me the importance of finding—and keeping—good team members. He told me that the most important decision he'd made as a professional was picking his first team member. That person was still a vital part of the business decades later. I quizzed him on how he managed his team, how he kept them focused on the big picture, and how he helped them maintain enthusiasm through long-range projects.

One of the most important things, he said, was never starting a meeting—whether it involved just one other person or the entire company—with a negative. Even if something had gone badly wrong, even if the meeting was about the thing that had gone wrong, he always started by asking everyone what had gone right. Specifically, he opened his meetings by saying, "Tell me something good."

> Even very simple things can have a huge impact upon how people feel and thus how they perform.

"Once you start talking about mistakes or problems or criticisms, people can go on forever about that," he said. "I'm never worried that we won't get to those things. But if we don't prioritize the good in life, we might miss it."

I had to laugh: here was the CEO of Life Is Good telling me to look on the bright side. Talk about being on-brand!

I took Jacobs's advice to heart—and not just in professional spaces. I realized that his philosophy of making good, positive things his first priority had suffused his whole life and business. It was what made him successful, but, more importantly, it was what made him happy. I started setting aside time to track my own wins at the end of each day, sort of an informal meeting with myself. Not only did it encourage me to reflect thoughtfully on the day—always a challenge for a busy person with a lot of stressors to manage—but it also forced me to put the most positive parts of my day in the clearest focus.

The wins didn't always have to be huge accomplishments. A win could be something as simple as having a chance to catch up with a friend over coffee, or telling a joke that cracked my wife up. I eventually settled on picking three wins each day and writing them down; that part of the process has kept me focused and motivated. Even on the worst day, when it feels like the world has constantly thrown roadblocks at me, I still sit down and find three successes to celebrate and record. When I look back on these "diary entries," I see a history of positives—a sequence of all the good parts of my life.

It is very easy to get an image of ourselves or our careers stuck in our heads. If that image is unhealthy or negative, it can create a destructive feedback loop where we see nothing but failure because we're constantly telling ourselves that we're going to fail. Consciously looking at the positives prevents me from falling into that trap and also gives me something to build on. Jacobs was right to highlight the positive in his meetings—not only for all the reasons

I've mentioned, but also because focusing too intensely on flaws, errors, mistakes, and failures is rarely energizing or productive. Of course, we have to talk about problems if we want to find solutions, but it's very easy to overdose on faultfinding, to your detriment. If you are constantly brooding over everything you've done wrong, that hardly makes you want to go out and tackle some new project.

I've incorporated Dan Sullivan's Three Wins™ model into every part of my life, often starting casual conversations with, "What were your three wins today?" It's an effective icebreaker because people rarely get asked that question, so they don't have stock responses and have to think a little deeper. People always answer, though, and they are often pleased to have a rare opportunity to reflect on what has gone right.

I've found that it's an especially good conversational gambit with kids, who are used to being asked general questions like, "How was school?" by adults who don't necessarily care very much about the answers. When you ask a seven- or eight-year-old a sincere question about his or her life, however, you get some illuminating answers. I've heard everything from, "I went across the monkey bars by myself" to "Mom let me flip the pancakes" to "I touched a turtle." As someone who doesn't have kids, I love these moments because they put my own model of what counts as a "success" or "failure" into perspective. How bad could any day really be if you got to touch a turtle?

Changing our language is an attempt, ultimately, to redo our internal color palette. If we change the way we talk about something, and keep at it, we will eventually change the way we think about that thing. It's a vital part of setting our color palette because one of the most important environments we have to manage is the one inside ourselves. Just as with our physical environment, we can dramatically alter our internal atmosphere by changing what may feel like small details. And, like the color we don't consciously realize is making us feel calmer or happier or slightly nauseous, we can be strongly affected by internal changes we might not have even consciously noticed.

Back in 2011, I was diagnosed with what turned out to be a pretty extreme case of sleep apnea, a condition that caused me to stop breathing periodically while I slept. Lots of things can cause sleep apnea, from excess weight to neurological issues, but the most common problem involves the physical structure of the throat and mouth. The lack of oxygen is disruptive enough to wake you (or at least to pull you from more restful sleep into shallower, fitful sleep) but often not shocking enough that you become fully conscious. Most people learn they have sleep apnea because of how they feel in the daytime: excessively tired, unfocused, moody, and all the other negative effects that come from lack of sleep.

I was being affected by sleep apnea long before I saw a doctor about the issue. But in my case, it was hard to separate the symptoms from my life in general. Like many people with ADHD, I'd always had problems with sleep. Insomnia and ADHD are highly comorbid, and I frequently wouldn't be able to sleep until three or four in the morning. I knew that I wasn't getting the recommended amount of sleep in a given night, so it never seemed all that unusual or worrisome when I experienced the symptoms of sleep deprivation. In fact, the longer it went on, the more it just began to feel like my natural state.

After my sleep apnea was discovered, I started using a CPAP machine and I was really pleased with the changes I noticed. Even on nights when I stayed up late, I was still feeling more rested in the morning than I would have otherwise. But a CPAP machine is a treatment, not a cure, and I started visiting different specialists in an attempt to figure out what caused my sleep apnea and how I might fix it in a more permanent way. Eventually, I met with an excellent maxillofacial surgeon here in Boston, Dr. Willie Stephens, who recommended an operation that would actually move my jaw forward and eliminate the physical structure in my face and throat that was causing my sleep apnea. It was a pretty intense prospect, but the surgeon was confident that it would essentially resolve my sleep problem.

The surgery took thirteen hours, and my body took six months to fully recover. I now have thirty-seven screws and five titanium plates in my skull and, although my wife swears I look just the same, I think my profile is subtly different. As dramatic as that change in my appearance sounds, however, it pales compared to the effect it had on my sleep. Immediately after the surgery, I went from having a 72 percent nighttime oxygen level to a 90 percent level, and it only improved from there.

Before the surgery, I had been in a really rough place with my business. I was so dissatisfied with how I was operating every day; I felt so unfocused and I was struggling constantly to stay on top of everything. I was actually thinking seriously about selling the company because I thought it had grown beyond my fundamental ability to manage it. I was actively, even aggressively, pursuing that option right up until the day of the surgery.

Then, the night before the operation, I had a great conversation with my doctor. We had developed a nice rapport in the weeks leading up to the surgery, and he knew all about my problems with the company.

"Scott," he told me, "I wouldn't sell your company. When you recover from this surgery, you are going to be on rocket fuel and you're going to feel differently about a lot of things."

I thought that sounded like a nice idea, but I wasn't sure how much I believed him. After the surgery, I understood completely. Getting enough sleep is one of things that we all "know" is good for us, but when you go from truly dysfunctional sleep to getting (mostly) a solid eight hours a night, it is transformational. My mind was so much more active and agile, I felt so much more capable, and things that had taken enormous amounts of energy before became relatively easy. I did feel like I was on rocket fuel! I felt like the sun had come up, the day had begun, and I was ready for action.

The change in me also manifested in my professional life. Rather than selling the company, I actually expanded it several times over. One year after the surgery, I was happily running a company that was larger and more complex than I ever could have imagined before.

Sleep is foundational, like breathing and eating, and, because it is so basic and so fundamental to our lives, it's easy to lose track of it. It's a lot like color in that way. Most of us don't consciously notice the colors that surround us, especially if they've been the same for a long time. But just because a wall has always been painted yellow, doesn't mean it can't be repainted. It certainly doesn't mean that painting it blue would be better for your productivity. We have to look at our surroundings with a photographer's eye: we have to see the possibilities, not just the immediate realities.

There's so much in life that is out of our hands. If I want to get a certain shot at blue hour, I'd better hustle and get in the right position at the right moment, because if I miss that moment through some sort of accident or calamity, I'll have to wait until tomorrow to try again. The revolution of the earth around the sun is always the same and we can't change it; we can only take advantage of the special moments when they come around. So what do we do? We control the things we can control. We plan and gather materials. We build teams and change our approach in response to success or failure.

> Taking charge of what we can control gives us the best possible chance to overcome what we can't.

That's how I think of managing our color palette: taking charge of things we can control to give us the best possible chance to overcome those things we can't. We can't make the sun rise or set—but we can make sure we are in the best possible position to capitalize on it.

CHAPTER 13

– Memory –
What Do You Store and
What Do You Ignore?

As you can probably tell by now, photography is one of those disciplines that can require a lot of tackle. Lenses, meters, tripods . . . we've talked about some of the tools photographers use to get that elusive perfect shot, and after more than four decades of taking pictures, I've amassed a pretty big collection of them all. The one type of equipment I have in the greatest supply, however, has to be memory cards. I have dozens of them, dating back to some of the first ones I ever used when digital cameras first came into common use.

In one way, it makes sense that I'd have so many: memory cards can fill up fast and you never want to be caught without one. But I definitely don't keep all my cards for the sake of utility. I still have all the cards from some of the earliest digital cameras I have owned; they have a fraction of the capacity of a modern memory card and many of them wouldn't even work in the cameras I currently use. Even if they did work in my preferred camera, most of them are completely full. The photos on those cards are backed up and stored elsewhere—at least the ones I knew I wanted to keep—so why do I hang on to all those old bits of plastic?

It's partially the same impulse that leads us to keep ticket stubs to long-past concerts or clothes that no longer fit: we keep these objects because they symbolize or even spur fond memories for us. In the case of my memory cards, they quite literally hold images from my past. Looking back at each card is like opening a time capsule: I can see not only the work I produced, but also the experiences I had. Going through the cards in sequence allows me to trace the evolution of my skills and practices as well as my interests over the years.

Most people don't use memory cards that way. Generally, people treat them like tools. They are designed to store images, and when they no longer do that effectively, people trade up to a newer or better version. When they fill up, people wipe them clean and start over. I've never erased a memory card and reused it, and I have seventeen years' worth of cards to prove it. Neither approach is the only correct one; people work differently and we all develop strategies to maximize our success.

I do think, though, that my hoarding of memory cards in contrast to the way they are typically used highlights something important about memory as a concept (outside of the computer). We all make choices about what we hold on to, what we memorialize, and what we wipe away to rebuild upon. Memory isn't just a passive concept; it's something that we do.

It's also an important concept to me because, like many photographers, I am in the business of memory-making. What is event photography but forging and recording physical mementos to help us later recall important moments in the past? Also, as someone with ADHD, my relationship to memory is a little different than the average person's. ADHD is associated particularly with poor working memory, sometimes called "short-term memory." The easiest way to describe working memory is that it's your ability to hold information in your head long enough to act on it. For example, if you are cooking a particular meal, you need to remember that you have to add half a cup of chopped onions when the water comes to a boil, but you really only need to recall that information as you are acting on it. Four hours later, you can—and probably will—forget everything about the recipe. But while you are actually using the information, it's as clear to you as your most cherished childhood memory. At least, that's how it's supposed to work.

For people with ADHD, working memory is often impaired. That's why we can struggle to complete tasks

> Memory isn't just a passive concept; it's something that we do.

or follow conversations or quickly get confused when attempting to follow directions. If you have ADHD and are preparing that same meal, you might need to check and recheck the recipe after every single step because you just can't remember the quantity of onions or when they go in the pot. Or you might forget about the onions entirely, and leave them sitting unchopped on the counter. And if anything occurs during the execution of the recipe, like you receive a text message or a knock at the door, all bets are off; you might even forget you were making food in the first place!

Interestingly, most studies show that ADHD doesn't seem to impact long-term memory. Long-term memory is essentially those things that we learn and store indefinitely. In the recipe example, the equivalent of a long-term memory might be remembering how to operate a stove, or it might be the sense memory you experience of your grandmother letting you chop vegetables with her when you were a kid. Procedural (memories of how to do things) and episodic (memories of moments or events) are types of long-term memories. When we make a memory like that, it literally changes the structure of our brains. Not only is long-term memory formation a physiological process, it's also one that is almost completely distinct from working memory. If working memory is like writing something on a whiteboard, long-term memory is like chiseling it into stone.

A person with ADHD can recall important moments, learn skills and repeat them, and even memorize facts about their passions just as well as—sometimes even better than—a "normal" person. Unfortunately, I've found that the contrast between working memory and long-term memory often causes more frustration and confusion than anything else. Memory is something that even scientists don't fully understand, so we can't really expect the average person to comprehend the differences between working and long-term memories or how they are formed in the brain, or even that they are separate functions. Most people believe that if you can remember an article you read five years ago, you should be able to remember to put the egg carton back in the fridge when you're done with it.

Remembering small details and being able to perform regular tasks are, for better or worse, two of the main ways we show people that we love and care for them. We often equate remembering something with caring about that thing, when, in reality, that's just not how our brain works. For example, my wife used to be totally baffled that I would go to the grocery store and come back without food for our dogs—sometimes even when I'd gone there specifically to pick that up!

"How could you forget about them?" she'd ask, knowing how much I loved our dogs. From my perspective, I wasn't forgetting about the dogs; I was failing to hold all the items on the grocery list in my head at one time. I could have forgotten the orange juice or left one of the grocery bags in the cart, and it would have been a result of the very same memory dysfunction. Certainly, it wasn't a measure of how much I cared about those items; if I'd been able to do so, I wouldn't have forgotten anything at all.

As the people around me and I have learned more about ADHD and how it works, we've changed some of our thinking about memory. We understand things differently now, but even with that extra knowledge, it's hard to stop a knee-jerk reaction. It's a little like having a loved one who is dealing with Alzheimer's disease or dementia in that both force us to confront the physiological workings of memory. Often, it's difficult and painful for everyone involved. We know logically that when people who have Alzheimer's disease forget our name or a conversation we had recently, it doesn't mean that they don't love us or cherish the time they've spent with us. It means their brains are changing and are no longer able to encode and retrieve information in the same way. When our mother or father remembers the name of a dog our sister had in 1986 but keeps mistaking us for the mail carrier, it can feel like a slight, even though we have enough knowledge about the disease to know that it's not. That is one of my biggest struggles with memory—not just forgetting important details, but also making sure that people don't feel like they are unimportant because I've forgotten those details.

Maybe that's part of the reason I am so big on keeping my memories safe and sound on an array of storage devices. My own brain is a bit of a faulty memory card—it can't be relied upon to store everything safely—so I need lots of backup. Maybe, too, it's part of the reason I was drawn to event photography. I love the idea of being able to create a physical object that does the work of memory. I love the idea of helping people demonstrate just how much they cherish their family and friends.

Here's another fun fact about memory: it is changed and shaped by the act of remembering. Each time we recall something, we change it subtly; that changed version is stored again in our long-term memory. This means that, after the first time something happens, we are no longer remembering that specific incident; we are remembering our memory of that incident. As we get further away from the initial event and remember it again and again, those small changes add up and can sometimes substantially change our understanding of our own memory. If you've ever been with a group of people and tried to recall a shared experience, you've probably seen this phenomenon in action. Two people almost never remember an event the exact same way. There might be small differences, like one person believing something happened at night, while the other insists it happened during the day. Or there might be big discrepancies, like a disagreement about who was present, what was said, or what actually happened.

A photograph, though, is always itself. You're never going to look through a photo album and find that a person has been added or subtracted from a picture, or the whole scene has moved to another state. A photograph is (at least compared to our memories) empirical evidence.

Of course, almost every chapter in this book has contained at least some information about how to shape and manipulate an image. We make choices about what to photograph, how to photograph it, what settings to use, and what visual elements to highlight. Finally, we make choices about which images to preserve and which images we let drift away. There's no such thing as a perfect memory, not even through a camera lens, and, oddly enough, that's a comforting thought.

Here's another fun fact: memory is changed and shaped by the act of remembering.

Perhaps because I'm someone with a noticeably flawed memory, I like the idea that there's not really any perfect truth when it comes to recalling the past. It reminds me that we actually have a lot of control over our memories and that it is what we choose to do with them, about them, and for them that matters the most.

Bob, a friend I'd been close to since childhood, passed away several years ago. Bob and I were kindred spirits in a lot of ways. We both loved photography and dreamed of expanding it into a business, and, while he was never diagnosed with ADHD, we shared many of its traits. Bob was who you picture when you think about a hyperactive person: he was always on the move, always throwing out ideas and running here and there, keeping a hand in everything that was going on. He was so active and energetic and spent so much time building his future that the last thing you would have thought of when you looked at him was, "This is a sick man." But that's the thing about cancer: it doesn't announce itself. Instead, it grows quietly in the dark until one day when it becomes strong enough to take your knees out from under you.

Bob and I shared office space and were both working toward establishing ourselves professionally, so we would constantly bounce ideas off each other. Often, we'd get so deep in conversation about how to solve one problem or another that we'd spend the whole afternoon talking and not completing any tasks. So we decided to save up all our ideas and questions and brain-picking requests, for a specific time and place: three in the afternoon at a nearby coffee shop. There, we'd load up on caffeine and go over whatever was on our minds. Bob was great for this kind of conversation because he would throw out whatever ideas came to him. He never self-censored about what seemed practical or sensible, and that often meant he came up with solutions that an average office team would have taken months to discover. He was also relentlessly upbeat. He really believed that we were both going to realize our visions.

Shortly before Bob was diagnosed with pancreatic cancer, we both took a trip out to Austin, Texas, to meet with

Graham McFarland. I'd long admired Graham's work, and I'd met him before and spoken to him on the phone, but this was Bob's first opportunity to meet him. In person, Graham was thoughtful and insightful, and the three of us had a great conversation.

That night, however, Bob got really sick. He hadn't been feeling quite right for a while and I knew that he had health problems, but that was the first time I'd actually seen him have an episode. For me, it was a turning point. I realized something then that I think Bob had known for a while: something was seriously wrong.

I wasn't sure that Bob had been formally diagnosed then but I think we both knew, though neither of us said it, that something terrible was happening to him. I helped him as much as I could and I didn't pry into the issue because I figured Bob would tell me what he wanted to tell me. The next day, we drove out to Dallas to catch our flight and Bob was mostly normal—a little grayer, a little more tired, but he was a version of the Bob that I knew. Then, during that long stretch of aimless Texan landscape, he turned to me and said, "Graham's a good guy. He's going to be in your life for a long time; I can tell."

It felt weirdly like a prophecy or even a blessing. There was a strangeness to how he said it, the way you talk to your friends from high school on the eve of everyone going off to college. It was like Bob realized we were in one of those last moments before everything changes. Those occur all the time, and, for the most part, we only realize it in retrospect. It is a gift, in a sense, to be aware that you're on the precipice of a new way of living and to be able to mark the occasion.

"Yeah," I said finally, "I think you're right."

Not long after we got back, Bob told me he had pancreatic cancer. It was advanced and aggressive, and his treatment options were limited. He was only forty years old.

I took some time off work to spend with him. We went fishing. We had long talks. We did just about everything we would have done if he weren't sick. That was how Bob wanted it; his illness made him even more determined to work toward our visions with whatever time he had left. He even still met me for three o'clock coffee as often as he could. A lot of the time, it was hard to believe that my friend was dying. I rarely saw him in his lowest moments, as I had in Austin, and when he was having a good day, he was so much like the old Bob that I could almost fool myself into thinking it was all some sort of crazy medical mistake. Maybe next week, he'd go back to the doctor and find out it was a case of misdiagnosis and there was nothing wrong with him at all.

But, of course, that didn't happen. Bob died shortly after being diagnosed. I've heard people say that there's no real preparation for the death of a loved one, even if you know for months or years in advance. That's certainly true, but there was still something about the abruptness of Bob's passing that made it feel particularly surreal. The day after he died, I went to the office by myself to collect some things. There, on the edge of my desk, was his coffee cup, with a little puddle of coffee still in the bottom. It looked like he had just left it there before ducking out to go to the bathroom or something. It looked like he was coming right back.

It was so weird to me that someone could be such a vibrant part of the world one day, and then completely vanish the next. There were so many empty spaces where he used to be. I found myself jotting down things to tell him later or heading to the coffee shop and half expecting to see him sitting there waiting for me. I still kept our three o'clock coffee appointments, but I missed having someone there who could discuss ideas with me. The first time I put out an open call for people to join me for three o'clock coffee, it was a spur-of-the-moment idea; I just wanted to talk to someone the way I'd talked to Bob.

Eventually, I made three o'clock coffee a regular part of my routine. I would put out a call on social media, offering my time to anyone who wanted to chat. The more of these conversations I had, the more I realized that not only did I get something from the interaction, I also had something to offer. I could do what Bob did for me: I could brainstorm and listen and help others feel that they weren't alone in whatever they were trying to get off the ground.

I threw the door wide open, creating public invitations on Facebook, Twitter, and even the Foursquare page of the Starbucks I went to. Some days, I had coffee with homeless people or heroin addicts; some days I met with CEOs. I met with old friends and total strangers, people who wanted to learn about starting a business or photography, or people who just liked coffee. Every coffee meeting was worthwhile. I heard some of the most amazing stories from the most surprising people. I puzzled over real, tricky problems, and even got some feedback on my work that was very useful.

I never go into a three o'clock meeting with an agenda other than to sit and have a conversation with another person. I don't want to sell anything or network (at least not in the mercenary sense most people imagine), and I'm not trying to get anything from the other person. All I want is to have a conversation, human to human, and enjoy that sense of connection. I still do this; in fact, if you're ever in Boston and need a caffeine fix around three o'clock, feel free to look me up.

Even now, years later, I still think about Bob whenever I have a coffee meeting. My memories of Bob aren't static; they're active. I remember him by sharing with others one of the most important parts of our friendship. In this way, I keep him with me just like I keep all my old memory cards because I never want to forget what he meant to me and how he helped make me the person I am today. Forgetting, as I see it, isn't just about losing details or mixing up facts; it's also about failing to act on our memories and keep them present in our daily lives. Put it this way: I might forget when to add the onions or preheat the oven, but if I make the same meal for Sunday dinner that my grandma always made, I am "remembering" her perfectly.

CHAPTER 14

– Resolution –
Seeing Things More Clearly

The average person hears about resolution most commonly in the context of screens—a computer monitor or television, for example. Most people have a general understanding that higher resolution equals better quality. But "resolution" is actually just a general term that refers simply to the level of visible detail in any image, whether it is reproduced on a computer screen or in a traditional photograph. It is generally true that resolution is often used as shorthand for image quality in photography. A low-resolution image contains a lot of that undesirable noise we talked about in the ISO chapter, and a *really* low-res image has so much noise that the actual image is obscured.

Resolution isn't a monolith though. Even within the realm of photography, there are a few different ways to talk

> Higher resolution equals better quality.

about resolution—and different ways to measure what is a somewhat elusive quality. For digital images, we can use the density of the pixels to grade the resolution. A pixel, in photography terms, is the smallest isolatable element of an image. The way I like to think about it is in terms of pointillism. You know those pictures made up of thousands upon thousands of individual dots of color? Pixels are essentially like that. If you think about a pointillist painting, you'll remember how from far away the overall image is more visually comprehensible. As you get closer to the canvas, you eventually begin to see it as a series of colorful dots. This is essentially true of pixel-based resolution as well; the more pixels you can pack into a square inch of image, the more it looks like a comprehensible shape, while the fewer pixels you have, the grainier and more abstract it becomes.

Pixels are an element of digital images, however, not analog ones. So when we talk about the resolution of images taken with traditional film, it all gets a bit more complicated. Analog film quality is often measured in line pairs, which are, as the name implies, pairs of one black and one white line. The resolution of analog film is a factor of how many of those pairs you can visually distinguish in one millimeter of a final image. It is possible to convert one measurement into another, but there's always a little bit of guesswork involved because film is prone to fluctuations in resolution quality depending on the camera settings, the development process, and other environmental factors. It's very hard to determine any equivalence between film and digital resolutions because they are such fundamentally different ways of presenting digital information; it's a little bit like asking how many inches equate to a temperature of twenty degrees. That hasn't stopped people from trying to make the comparison, however, and the average 35 mm film is often said to have roughly the equivalent quality of a 20-megapixel digital photo.

The quest for better image quality—and thus a higher resolution—has been one of the primary drivers of innovation in photography since the first techniques for recording camera images were developed in the early 1800s. The camera itself was created long before we developed the ability to record the images seen via the device. The word comes from *camera obscura*—a Latin term generally translated as "dark room" or "dark chamber"—and some of the earliest versions were, in fact, just dark rooms. You may also have heard the term "pinhole camera"; the two are basically synonymous.

Basically, you take a box and poke a small hole in it (or, in the oldest versions, you drill a small hole in one wall of an otherwise sealed and lightless room). Because light travels in straight lines, a small hole can isolate specific rays of light (in this case, those given off by an object), and those rays of light then travel through that reduced space and hit some sort of backstop. In a boxed camera obscura, this would be the blank wall of the box or the room. The interior of the box has to be completely dark so that the only light is what comes through the small hole. The hole focuses and isolates the image, and, if done correctly, reflects it onto the far surface.

For a long time, this technique was used to do things like viewing eclipses, which would otherwise cause eye damage if observed directly. The same principle was even used in astronomy and architecture to create meaningful image projections when the sun or moon was in a specific position over the building. Probably the most common example of a camera obscura, however, is in our very own eyes. The pupil is the pinhole, the retina is the projection surface, and the material of the eye itself is the "dark room." Considering that we carry these cameras around with us all the time, it makes sense that this would be a technology that humans mastered fairly early on. In fact, there's evidence to suggest that the camera obscura principle (if not the device as we would recognize it) existed in cultures as geographically and temporally far-flung as Paleolithic Europe, Ancient China, and first-century Egypt.

The birth of photography came about, however, when we started trying to permanently capture those images produced by a camera. *Cameras obscuras* were popular tools for artists, especially painters, who would use them to project images from life onto a surface and trace or etch them. Around the year 1800, people began experimenting with chemical substances that reacted to light, particularly silver nitrate.

The general approach involved coating a surface (usually paper or fabric, but sometimes metal plates) with some reactive substance (silver chloride, bitumen, the aforementioned silver nitrate) and projecting an image onto it using a camera obscura. The light parts of the image would spark the chemical reaction, changing the color or texture of that part of the surface, while the dark areas where no light was expressed would cause no reaction. The result was, more or less, a permanent record of what was previously just a fleeting visual moment.

There were a lot of downsides to this method. First of all, you often wound up with an unwieldy metal plate instead of something more portable and useful. Also, it took a long time. The earliest extant example of this kind of photography (called *View from the Window at Le Gras*) probably took inventor Nicéphore Niépce days of exposure. Most importantly, the image quality was not very good. If you look at *View from the Window at Le Gras*, it's extremely fuzzy, filled with what we would today call "noise." The shapes of buildings and the surrounding countryside are only barely distinguishable in the haze, but it still represented the beginning of an entirely new type of art. Soon, the race was on to develop a more convenient system that produced clearer and sharper images.

In the 1830s came the daguerreotype, copper plates covered in silver, which were then buffed to a high polish. Exposure was accomplished with a "mercury vapor," and the plates were usually sealed under glass to prevent them from tarnishing or cracking when exposed to air. It was the first widely available photographic process, and, because of that, innovations, improvements, and advances came fast and furious in the years after the daguerreotype's introduction. People experimented with different types of plates and reactive chemicals, and they attempted to reduce the exposure time to get more and more fine detail in the final image plate.

It's rare to find a true daguerreotype from that period in good condition, both because many other similar but later types of prints are often mistaken for daguerreotypes and because many were not stored in a way that kept them protected. There is some evidence that a good daguerreotype done by a professional could have a resolution that modern digital cameras could only dream about. In 2010, *Wired* reported on the restoration of some panoramic daguerreotypes dating back to 1848: "Finally, the conservators deployed a stereo microscope. What they saw astonished them: The details—down to window curtains and wheel spokes—remained crisp even at 30X magnification. The panorama could be blown up to 170 by 20 feet without losing clarity; a digicam would have to record 140,000 megapixels per shot to match that."[3]

3 Julie Rehmeyer, "1848 Daguerreotypes Bring Middle America's Past to Life," *Wired*, July 9, 2010, https://www.wired.com/2010/07/ff_daguerrotype_panorama/.

One of the main ways people got that high resolution was by changing the surfaces they used to capture the camera images. Glass plates came into vogue around 1850 because, unlike the thin metal plates, they didn't bend and warp. Glass plates were also capable of capturing an enormous amount of detail. One of the big drawbacks, however, was the size. If you wanted to capture a larger item or scene, you would get a better resolution with a larger plate. Obviously, this put a ceiling on how much detail you could get in your big shots.

A famous aerial photographer named George R. Lawrence once attempted to push the limits of the issue with a truly enormous camera called "The Mammoth Camera." He designed and commissioned it specifically to photograph the Alton Limited, a new train from the Chicago & Alton Railway. The company had actually sought Lawrence out after seeing his revolutionary panoramas of postearthquake San Francisco, and they offered him a blank check to make the largest photograph ever—of their train. The result was displayed at the 1900 Paris Exposition as well as hyped relentlessly in the Chicago & Alton Railway's publicity materials. The Mammoth Camera allegedly weighed about 1,400 pounds and Lawrence had to get a specially designed ladder to operate it. It had to be so huge because it was designed to hold an eight-by-four-foot glass image plate, the largest image plate that had ever been manufactured.

Under the right conditions, glass plates offered a lot of detail and clarity, but they were a fussy and delicate tool.

The high quality of the images, though, kept glass in use for a long time. For certain specialized photographic needs like medical imaging and astronomical photography, it was preferred well into the modern era, and some of you may have seen glass negatives used by older photographers. Eventually, though, the need for a more accessible, more convenient option led inevitably to film.

One of the earliest widespread types of photographic film was nitrate film, which was made from nitrocellulose. It was flexible, convenient, and easily mass produced. Unfortunately, it was also highly flammable, didn't need oxygen to keep burning, and decayed in a chemically unpredictable way. Cellulose acetate film was soon developed as a "safer" alternative, but while it was less flammable, it still decayed erratically, giving off toxic, vinegar-smelling gases. This new development didn't put nitrate film out of business, however. Despite being well aware of the risks associated with nitrate film, photographers continued to use it up until 1951. Many actually preferred it because they thought it offered finer detail, and, in particular, a richer contrast between light and dark.

Eventually, of course, digital cameras emerged and sidelined physical film of all varieties. Resolution, sensitivity, and image quality have been steadily improving since the development of the first digital camera. Each new model that hits the market aims for more pixels and greater sharpness. Just like the innovators of early photography, digital tinkerers are always looking for clearer, more faithful, and more beautiful images.

So why did I tell you all this? Well, in part because this is a book about a professional photographer. Did you really think you were going to get out of here without learning some photography fun facts? But also because I wanted to highlight the importance of process and not just when it comes to technology. The story of how we achieved modern photographic resolution is, in many ways, a resolution of its own. Each piece (or "picture element," if you prefer) falls into place one at a time, and gradually, all the pieces cohere into a whole.

When we think about resolution, we often think about it as a sense of resolve, like making a new year's resolution. We think about voicing an intention and following through on it—making something happen, essentially. But I would also like you to think about resolution in the sense of an image: what pieces have to be present to make an image clear? How are our visions made up of dozens—or hundreds—of smaller steps and decisions?

The story I just told you—how image resolution was understood, developed, and refined—all happened in a little over two hundred years, and it was far from a linear progression. That is also the story of most successful people; even the most dramatic success story usually has years or decades of forward and back, false starts, and detours behind it. Most change is incremental, yet that can be one of the most difficult things to accept, especially in our professional lives, where more than anything, we want a clear forward momentum to validate all the risks we've taken.

When we take what we believe is a step forward (say, developing a new kind of flexible film that offers a luxurious quality to images not seen in other media), it can be incredibly demoralizing to realize that we have forgotten a piece of the puzzle (for example, discovering that our new wonder film might spontaneously combust when stored in less-than-perfect conditions). It can feel like the work is never-ending and we can see that horizon drifting further and further away.

And then there are the pieces that change the character of the whole puzzle. For photographic resolution, it might be something like *View from the Window at Le Gras*, which showed everyone that actually recording camera images was even possible. For me personally, it would be something like my ADHD diagnosis, which forced me to reassess almost everything about my life and my work. Is it starting over when you get one of those pieces that changes your assessment of what is possible? It certainly can feel like it a lot of the time.

Even the seeming setbacks give us more information about our ultimate goal though. Nitrate film introduced chemical concepts that were successfully used with other, more stable materials. My diagnosis opened a whole world of new tools and strategies and changed what I imagined to be my own limitations. As with film resolution, the goal isn't just a pretty picture; the goal is to have more information (specifically visual information) in the picture. Working on your resolution means putting aside that final vision for just a moment and focusing on gathering information and learning as you go—knowing just a little bit more and doing just a little bit better all the time.

Do you know why we really think of image quality in terms of resolution? Because an image with more visual information is a truer image. It more accurately depicts whatever is being photographed, without the chaos introduced by the process of seeing and recording. The same is true of our personal resolution: the more we learn about ourselves and our stated goals, the more accurately we will be able to describe and visualize those goals.

When I was seven years old and helping my father in the darkroom, I already in a sense wanted what I want today: I wanted to make photography my life's work. What has changed between then and now is all resolution: pixels, lines, light, and shade all falling into place. Back then, my idea of what it meant to pursue my passion for photography was as hazy as the view out of Nicéphore Niépce's window: I could see some vague contours, but there was so much I was just guessing about. Over the years, I have slowly but surely added to my sense of what I really want and how that life would look. It is like the experience would be of sharpening that image until you could see sun glinting off the raindrops on those long-ago French rooftops.

The search for resolution—like the search for clarity, fidelity, and understanding in any other part of life—is also something that never really ends. We have to embrace incremental changes and a puzzle-piece approach to building our futures—because if there's one thing we can learn from the history of photographic technology, it's that there's always a way to get to more. My vision for my business and goals for my future have changed not only because I've learned more about the industry, but also because the industry has changed so much, even just in my lifetime. Who can say if the goals we have today will even make sense—or seem all that aspirational—in ten or fifteen years? If George R. Lawrence had been a few decades older, would he have bothered making the world's largest glass imaging plate, or would he have instead been experimenting with film?

I suspect that, like most of the best innovators and artists, he would have been gathering all the information he could about his industry, adapting, and adjusting as that ever-changing picture kept resolving before him.

> The search for resolution—like the search for clarity, fidelity, and understanding in any other part of life—is also something that never really ends.

CHAPTER 15

What Does a Photograph Mean?

For a kid who is maybe seven or eight, just on the far edge of that magic time when anything seems possible, a picture taken with Santa Claus might be indisputable proof that the stories are real. For that's kid's parents, it might be an adorable record of a holiday spent together. For that kid's jaded thirteen-year-old brother, it might be embarrassing evidence of the sorts of uncool family bonding activities his parents demand. For a child living in poverty who hasn't ever had the chance to visit Santa before, it's a celebration of a time when someone listened to him and asked him what he wanted as though he had all the options in the world. Even the most straightforward picture can be an optical illusion, changing depending on who is doing the looking—and the circumstances under which they are doing that looking.

> Even the most straightforward picture can be an optical illusion.

Almost twenty years ago now, I had the opportunity to photograph the premiere of the second *Harry Potter* movie. When the offer first came in, I actually had no idea what the person was talking about; I thought Harry Potter was some actor who'd flown under my radar or maybe some figure they were doing a biopic on. I didn't have kids and I didn't really have the patience or focus yet for much reading, so the whole phenomenon had pretty much passed me by, a fact that seemed to shock the Warner Bros. rep who called me.

"You really don't know who Harry Potter is?" he asked.

"I really don't."

"Wow," he marveled, before giving me a crash course on the globally popular boy wizard. It actually sounded pretty cool when I'd heard all the details.

The event I would be photographing was an early American preview, before the film opened wide across the country. It was an extremely high-profile event, the kind that is usually photographed by an in-house team, especially for a big studio like Warner Bros. At the time I received this call, however, we were only about a year out from 9/11, and as the man on the phone explained to me, the film crew wasn't comfortable going to a highly visible event in New York via plane at that time. Because they knew I was in Boston and could drive to New York, they decided to reach out to me.

In Boston, like a lot of places on the East Coast (and probably throughout the rest of the country), the fallout from September 11 was everywhere. It felt both far away and painfully close. One of my parents' neighbors, a man named John Ogonowski was the pilot on American Airlines Flight 11, one of the planes that were flown into the twin towers. John was murdered that day; it seemed surreal that a nice, ordinary guy my family had known for years could die in such a shocking and horrible way. That surreal feeling was kind of a micro version of how the whole attack felt to a lot of people in the area: John wasn't the kind of guy who got murdered, and New York wasn't the kind of city where terrorists killed thousands of people.

But both had happened, and we were all left to find a way to make sense of it.

I could understand the film crew's reservations. Nothing felt certain; everything felt upside down. Who could say what was safe and what was not anymore? After all, we'd all behaved as though America were safe from that kind of violence, and we had been proven dramatically wrong. Still, I didn't want to be afraid of New York or of being at highly visible events—I wanted that to be my business, after all—so I immediately accepted the job.

The premiere was a little subdued, but it was still a movie premiere, and for one of the biggest properties in the world at that time (though it may not have been so big among the thirty-something professional-photographer demographic).

There were tons of people present, some famous and some not, and I had set up my Photos in a Minute system to take and print photos on demand for any guest who wanted one. The technology I was using was still a little new to me at the time, and I was really enjoying the process.

I was floating around, going from station to station to make sure everything was running smoothly and that all the equipment was in order, when I noticed Robin Williams and a boy I presumed to be his son looking curiously at one of my setups. Now, I may not have known my Dumbledores from my Voldemorts, but I most certainly knew who Robin Williams was; he had been a fixture of film and TV comedy since I was a kid. He had also just starred in *One Hour Photo*, a dark thriller about a sinister photo-lab technician who becomes obsessed with a family while processing their pictures. It was considered a big artistic departure for him at the time—nothing about the role or the movie was funny at all—and he was praised for his performance. As a photographer, I'd naturally made a point of seeing the movie. I'd really liked it, and like a lot of people, I had been impressed by Williams's range and intensity.

I struck up a conversation with him about the equipment and how it worked, and told him how much I'd enjoyed *One Hour Photo*. He seemed a little surprised but pleased to hear me say it; I guess he wasn't expecting a lot of adult-thriller fans at the *Harry Potter* premiere. He asked me a few questions about the Photos in a Minute process, and I was happy to show him how it all worked. I even personally took the photo of him with his son.

As were chatting and waiting for his photo to print, however, someone apparently took the picture out of the printer before we could retrieve it. There were so many people and we were taking so many pictures that I don't know if someone genuinely confused his photo with their own and took it by mistake, or if someone saw a chance to get a personal picture of a star and leapt at it.

I do know what Robin thought, however. He was clearly concerned about the missing photo, and seemed especially angry because his son was in it. He was not in the practice of putting his kids in the spotlight in that way. Robin had come to the premiere for his son, who loved the books and wanted to see the movie . . . not as a star or a performer. I think he felt frustrated that someone had trespassed on his "dad time."

I quickly offered him another photo and ushered him and his son in front of the camera again. "Damn pricks," he muttered into my ear as we went. He said it with a joking tone, but he was clearly irritated. Someone swiping his photo had put a damper on his night, and though he could still joke and be personable, his demeanor had changed slightly. I got the sense he wasn't having fun anymore.

After we got the second picture safely out of the printer, I asked Robin if he would take a quick picture with me, and he gracefully agreed. It's a strange picture; he's wearing a big, thick rain jacket, even though it was a perfectly clear night, and while he was happy enough to take the photo with me, he didn't smile.

Or maybe it just looks odd to me considering everything that later happened to Robin Williams and the tragic way his life ended. Maybe I want to see a deeper sadness in him when in reality, he was just annoyed. If he were still alive and performing today, maybe I would see that picture as evidence of his eccentric, humorous sensibility rather than an indication of some unhappiness underneath the surface.

The plot of *One Hour Photo* (loosely speaking) is that a photo technician imagines this local family is perfect based on their pictures. He projects onto them all his longing for human connection and warmth and love, and when he sees something that complicates that story, he loses his mind. But of course, the family was never perfect in the ways he'd imagined. It was simply a story he'd told himself based on his assessments of mere snapshots in their lives.

So what is a photograph? Is it just a subjective interpretation of a moment? I tend to believe that photographs are stories. A photograph is a method of communication, a narrative that makes you think about one thing or another. I approached this book the way I approach my photography: I want to tell you stories, and to use those stories to highlight important ideas.

I've told you quite a bit now about how photographers shape and control their photographs to elicit certain reactions or emotional responses in the viewer. But what I haven't talked as much about is the part where we have to let go and put our work out into the world.

Finding "meaning" in a photo is a collaborative process. The photographs I've taken, like the stories in this book, might mean different things to different people depending on where they are in their lives. There may be ideas or themes in them that I'd never intended, but that nevertheless get passed along, and that's a good thing. I want you, the reader, to take from this book what you need and what will help

I wrote this book to tell you stories, and to use those stories to highlight important ideas.

you. If it's advice about building a company, that's great; if it's support for something challenging in your personal life, that's wonderful. If it's just a sense that you're not alone and other people are struggling with some of the same challenges and imperfections, that is perfect.

I've presented you with a series of pictures—a whole gallery's worth—and it's up to you to put them all together and find the story that makes sense for you.

CONCLUSION

The Lens Cap

I could not end this book without another camera metaphor. The lens cap has an important purpose: to protect your lens from damage. Whenever you travel with your camera equipment, you need to pay careful attention to be sure it is protected and that it will be ready for your next photo shoot.

And it's not just professional-quality DSLRs that require this kind of protection: the camera in your pocket—your smartphone—needs a sturdy phone case, an item that manufacturers produce in a variety of colors and fancy styles. Top manufacturers like Nikon, Canon, and Sony promote their brands by emblazoning their iconic logos on the front of their pro DSLR camera lens caps.

You might be wondering why I'm bringing up these facts about lens caps, but that's the wrong question to consider. There are two better questions you should ask yourself instead.

The first question is this: What are you doing to protect your most significant investment? I'm not talking about your camera lens, but rather, the eyes you see with and the mind that tells you what to focus on.

My father has always protected me and given me guidance. It all started the minute he focused his eyes on me (and perhaps his camera as well) in what I imagine was a perfect "Kodak moment" on that sweltering summer night in 1969 when I was born.

My dad has always been my "lens cap," protecting me from danger and making sure I had some way to overcome any obstacles that got in my way. Or perhaps he provided me with the lens cap I needed to stop the shining lights that can cause distractions in my life.

In the seventies, ADHD was not well understood and Adderall hadn't been invented yet. We didn't have the internet to search WebMD back then either, but somehow my dad figured it out and saw that I had "camera focus."

My dad's name is Lenny Proposki, and all his good friends call him "Len." That name, Len, makes it easy for me to think of him as my *lens* cap.

So a better way to phrase that first question might be, "Who's *your* lens cap?"

The second question you should ask yourself is, "Whose lens cap am *I*?"

Some of the most creative people in the world are individuals with ADD or ADHD. Perhaps you are one of them, or, more likely, you know someone with traits similar to those I've described in this book. You should ask yourself how you can be a lens cap to someone else, providing mentorship and coaching to help others focus on seeing the big picture.

My purpose in writing this book—to help others focus on seeing the big picture in business and in life—has now become my life's journey. I will continue to provide information on my website, www.camerafocus.com, about resources that can help others.

> Protect your most significant investment—the eyes you see with and the mind that tells you what to focus on.

The cameras we use are our tools. We are proud of our tools, and are happy to display their brand logos on our lens caps. Similarly, Strategic Coach provides me with the tools I need to organize my business and my life, and I'm proud to display them in this book. Like my father, they, too, serve as my lens cap—another tool, one that gives me the vision I need to imagine a bigger future ahead.

Find *your* lens cap so that you can make your future bigger.